50 Japan Premium Cookie Recipes for Home

By: Kelly Johnson

Table of Contents

- Sweet Red Bean and Matcha Cookies
- Kabocha (Japanese Pumpkin) and Spice Cookies
- Yuzu and Sesame Cookies
- Maple and Azuki Cookies
- Black Sugar Cookies
- Matcha and White Sesame Cookies
- Shiso and Almond Cookies
- Sweet Potato and Black Sesame Cookies
- Uji Matcha and White Chocolate Chip Cookies
- Katsuobushi (Dried Bonito Flakes) Cookies
- Cherry and Matcha Cookies
- Miso and Chocolate Cookies
- Wasabi and Cashew Cookies
- Yuzu Marmalade Cookies
- Sweet Red Bean and Chestnut Cookies
- Japanese Pear Cookies
- Kinako and Matcha Shortbread Cookies
- Japanese Chestnut and Ginger Cookies

Matcha Shortbread Cookies

Ingredients:

- 1 cup (2 sticks) unsalted butter, softened
- 1/2 cup granulated sugar
- 1/4 cup powdered sugar
- 2 cups all-purpose flour
- 2 tablespoons matcha green tea powder
- 1/4 teaspoon salt
- Optional: 1 teaspoon vanilla extract or almond extract

Instructions:

1. **Preheat Oven**: Preheat your oven to 350°F (175°C). Line a baking sheet with parchment paper or a silicone baking mat.
2. **Cream Butter and Sugars**: In a large bowl, beat the softened butter, granulated sugar, and powdered sugar together until light and fluffy. This usually takes about 2-3 minutes.
3. **Add Flavorings**: If using, mix in the vanilla or almond extract.
4. **Mix Dry Ingredients**: In a separate bowl, whisk together the flour, matcha powder, and salt.
5. **Combine**: Gradually add the dry ingredients to the butter mixture, mixing until just combined. The dough will be thick and somewhat crumbly.
6. **Shape the Cookies**: Turn the dough onto a lightly floured surface and gently knead it to bring it together. Roll out the dough to about 1/4-inch thickness. Use cookie cutters to cut out shapes, or simply slice the dough into rectangles if you prefer.
7. **Chill**: Place the cut-out cookies on the prepared baking sheet. If the dough is too soft, chill the cookies on the baking sheet in the refrigerator for about 15 minutes before baking.
8. **Bake**: Bake the cookies in the preheated oven for 10-12 minutes, or until the edges are just starting to turn golden brown.
9. **Cool**: Allow the cookies to cool on the baking sheet for a few minutes before transferring them to a wire rack to cool completely.
10. **Enjoy**: Store in an airtight container for up to a week.

These Matcha Shortbread Cookies are a delicious combination of buttery shortbread and earthy matcha, perfect for tea time or as a special treat!

Black Sesame Cookies

Ingredients:

- 1 cup (2 sticks) unsalted butter, softened
- 1/2 cup granulated sugar
- 1/4 cup powdered sugar
- 1 1/2 cups all-purpose flour
- 1/2 cup black sesame seeds, toasted
- 1/4 teaspoon salt
- Optional: 1 teaspoon vanilla extract

Instructions:

1. **Preheat Oven**: Preheat your oven to 350°F (175°C). Line a baking sheet with parchment paper or a silicone baking mat.
2. **Prepare Sesame Seeds**: Toast the black sesame seeds in a dry skillet over medium heat until fragrant, about 2-3 minutes. Let them cool completely before using.
3. **Cream Butter and Sugars**: In a large bowl, beat the softened butter, granulated sugar, and powdered sugar together until light and fluffy, about 2-3 minutes.
4. **Add Vanilla (Optional)**: Mix in the vanilla extract if using.
5. **Mix Dry Ingredients**: In a separate bowl, whisk together the flour and salt.
6. **Combine**: Gradually add the flour mixture to the butter mixture, mixing until just combined. Stir in the toasted black sesame seeds.
7. **Shape the Cookies**: Roll the dough into 1-inch balls and place them on the prepared baking sheet. Flatten each ball slightly with the back of a spoon or your fingers.
8. **Bake**: Bake in the preheated oven for 10-12 minutes, or until the edges are just beginning to turn golden brown.
9. **Cool**: Allow the cookies to cool on the baking sheet for a few minutes before transferring them to a wire rack to cool completely.
10. **Enjoy**: Store in an airtight container for up to a week.

These Black Sesame Cookies have a nutty, slightly sweet flavor and a delightful crunch, making them a unique and tasty treat!

Yuzu and White Chocolate Cookies

Ingredients:

- 1 cup (2 sticks) unsalted butter, softened
- 1/2 cup granulated sugar
- 1/4 cup brown sugar, packed
- 1 large egg
- 2 cups all-purpose flour
- 1/2 teaspoon baking soda
- 1/4 teaspoon salt
- 1/2 cup yuzu juice (fresh or bottled, available in Asian markets)
- 1 cup white chocolate chips or chunks
- Optional: 1 teaspoon vanilla extract

Instructions:

1. **Preheat Oven**: Preheat your oven to 350°F (175°C). Line a baking sheet with parchment paper or a silicone baking mat.
2. **Cream Butter and Sugars**: In a large bowl, beat the softened butter, granulated sugar, and brown sugar together until light and fluffy, about 2-3 minutes.
3. **Add Egg and Vanilla**: Beat in the egg and vanilla extract, mixing until well combined.
4. **Mix Dry Ingredients**: In a separate bowl, whisk together the flour, baking soda, and salt.
5. **Combine Ingredients**: Gradually add the dry ingredients to the butter mixture, mixing until just combined. Stir in the yuzu juice and white chocolate chips.
6. **Shape the Cookies**: Drop rounded tablespoons of dough onto the prepared baking sheet, spacing them about 2 inches apart. Flatten each dough ball slightly with the back of a spoon.
7. **Bake**: Bake in the preheated oven for 10-12 minutes, or until the edges are golden brown and the centers are set.
8. **Cool**: Allow the cookies to cool on the baking sheet for a few minutes before transferring them to a wire rack to cool completely.
9. **Enjoy**: Store in an airtight container for up to a week.

These Yuzu and White Chocolate Cookies offer a delightful blend of tart yuzu and sweet white chocolate, creating a unique and refreshing cookie experience.

Green Tea and Almond Cookies

Ingredients:

- 1 cup (2 sticks) unsalted butter, softened
- 1/2 cup granulated sugar
- 1/4 cup powdered sugar
- 1 3/4 cups all-purpose flour
- 2 tablespoons matcha green tea powder
- 1/2 cup sliced almonds
- 1/4 teaspoon salt
- Optional: 1 teaspoon vanilla extract

Instructions:

1. **Preheat Oven**: Preheat your oven to 350°F (175°C). Line a baking sheet with parchment paper or a silicone baking mat.
2. **Cream Butter and Sugars**: In a large bowl, beat the softened butter, granulated sugar, and powdered sugar together until light and fluffy, about 2-3 minutes.
3. **Add Vanilla (Optional)**: Mix in the vanilla extract if using.
4. **Mix Dry Ingredients**: In a separate bowl, whisk together the flour, matcha powder, and salt.
5. **Combine**: Gradually add the dry ingredients to the butter mixture, mixing until just combined. Stir in the sliced almonds.
6. **Shape the Cookies**: Roll the dough into 1-inch balls and place them on the prepared baking sheet. Flatten each ball slightly with the back of a spoon or your fingers, and press a few additional almond slices on top of each cookie for garnish.
7. **Bake**: Bake in the preheated oven for 10-12 minutes, or until the edges are just beginning to turn golden brown.
8. **Cool**: Allow the cookies to cool on the baking sheet for a few minutes before transferring them to a wire rack to cool completely.
9. **Enjoy**: Store in an airtight container for up to a week.

These Green Tea and Almond Cookies offer a delicious balance of green tea's subtle bitterness with the sweet crunch of almonds, making them a perfect treat for tea time or as a unique addition to your cookie collection.

Chestnut and Honey Cookies

Ingredients:

- 1 cup (2 sticks) unsalted butter, softened
- 1/2 cup granulated sugar
- 1/4 cup powdered sugar
- 1 3/4 cups all-purpose flour
- 2 tablespoons matcha green tea powder
- 1/2 cup sliced almonds
- 1/4 teaspoon salt
- Optional: 1 teaspoon vanilla extract

Instructions:

1. **Preheat Oven**: Preheat your oven to 350°F (175°C). Line a baking sheet with parchment paper or a silicone baking mat.
2. **Cream Butter and Sugars**: In a large bowl, beat the softened butter, granulated sugar, and powdered sugar together until light and fluffy, about 2-3 minutes.
3. **Add Vanilla (Optional)**: Mix in the vanilla extract if using.
4. **Mix Dry Ingredients**: In a separate bowl, whisk together the flour, matcha powder, and salt.
5. **Combine**: Gradually add the dry ingredients to the butter mixture, mixing until just combined. Stir in the sliced almonds.
6. **Shape the Cookies**: Roll the dough into 1-inch balls and place them on the prepared baking sheet. Flatten each ball slightly with the back of a spoon or your fingers, and press a few additional almond slices on top of each cookie for garnish.
7. **Bake**: Bake in the preheated oven for 10-12 minutes, or until the edges are just beginning to turn golden brown.
8. **Cool**: Allow the cookies to cool on the baking sheet for a few minutes before transferring them to a wire rack to cool completely.
9. **Enjoy**: Store in an airtight container for up to a week.

These Green Tea and Almond Cookies offer a delicious balance of green tea's subtle bitterness with the sweet crunch of almonds, making them a perfect treat for tea time or as a unique addition to your cookie collection.

Miso Caramel Cookies

Ingredients:

For the Cookies:

- 1 cup (2 sticks) unsalted butter, softened
- 1/2 cup granulated sugar
- 1/4 cup brown sugar, packed
- 1/4 cup white miso paste (preferably sweet white miso)
- 1 large egg
- 2 cups all-purpose flour
- 1/2 teaspoon baking soda
- 1/4 teaspoon salt
- Optional: 1 teaspoon vanilla extract

For the Caramel Drizzle:

- 1/2 cup caramel sauce (store-bought or homemade)
- Sea salt, for sprinkling (optional)

Instructions:

1. **Preheat Oven**: Preheat your oven to 350°F (175°C). Line a baking sheet with parchment paper or a silicone baking mat.
2. **Cream Butter and Sugars**: In a large bowl, beat the softened butter, granulated sugar, brown sugar, and miso paste together until light and fluffy, about 2-3 minutes.
3. **Add Egg and Vanilla**: Beat in the egg and vanilla extract (if using) until well combined.
4. **Mix Dry Ingredients**: In a separate bowl, whisk together the flour, baking soda, and salt.
5. **Combine Ingredients**: Gradually add the dry ingredients to the butter mixture, mixing until just combined.
6. **Shape the Cookies**: Drop rounded tablespoons of dough onto the prepared baking sheet, spacing them about 2 inches apart. Flatten each dough ball slightly with the back of a spoon.
7. **Bake**: Bake in the preheated oven for 10-12 minutes, or until the edges are golden brown and the centers are set.
8. **Cool and Drizzle**: Allow the cookies to cool on the baking sheet for a few minutes before transferring them to a wire rack to cool completely. Once cooled, drizzle the caramel sauce over the cookies and sprinkle with a pinch of sea salt if desired.
9. **Enjoy**: Store the cookies in an airtight container. They are best enjoyed fresh but can be stored for up to a week.

These Miso Caramel Cookies offer a delightful blend of sweet and savory flavors, making them a memorable treat for those who appreciate unique and sophisticated cookie recipes.

Sakura Blossom Cookies

Ingredients:

For the Cookies:

- 1 cup (2 sticks) unsalted butter, softened
- 1/2 cup granulated sugar
- 1/4 cup powdered sugar
- 2 cups all-purpose flour
- 1/4 teaspoon salt
- 2 tablespoons sakura (cherry blossom) extract or cherry blossom syrup (available in Asian markets)
- Optional: 1 teaspoon vanilla extract

For the Decoration:

- 1/4 cup edible sakura flower petals, dried and chopped (optional)
- 1/4 cup granulated sugar, for sprinkling (optional)

Instructions:

1. **Preheat Oven**: Preheat your oven to 350°F (175°C). Line a baking sheet with parchment paper or a silicone baking mat.
2. **Cream Butter and Sugars**: In a large bowl, beat the softened butter, granulated sugar, and powdered sugar together until light and fluffy, about 2-3 minutes.
3. **Add Flavorings**: Mix in the sakura extract or syrup and vanilla extract (if using).
4. **Mix Dry Ingredients**: In a separate bowl, whisk together the flour and salt.
5. **Combine Ingredients**: Gradually add the dry ingredients to the butter mixture, mixing until just combined.
6. **Shape the Cookies**: Roll the dough out on a lightly floured surface to about 1/4-inch thickness. Use cookie cutters to cut out shapes, or simply slice into squares if you prefer.
7. **Decorate**: If using, gently press a few chopped sakura petals into the tops of the cookies, or sprinkle with granulated sugar for added sparkle.
8. **Bake**: Bake in the preheated oven for 10-12 minutes, or until the edges are just beginning to turn golden brown.
9. **Cool**: Allow the cookies to cool on the baking sheet for a few minutes before transferring them to a wire rack to cool completely.
10. **Enjoy**: Store in an airtight container for up to a week.

These Sakura Blossom Cookies are a lovely way to celebrate the beauty of cherry blossoms, offering a subtle floral flavor that pairs beautifully with a cup of tea.

Soy Sauce and Ginger Cookies

Ingredients:

For the Cookies:

- 1 cup (2 sticks) unsalted butter, softened
- 1/2 cup granulated sugar
- 1/4 cup brown sugar, packed
- 1 large egg
- 1 tablespoon soy sauce (light soy sauce works best)
- 2 cups all-purpose flour
- 1 tablespoon ground ginger
- 1/2 teaspoon baking soda
- 1/4 teaspoon salt

For the Sugar Coating (Optional):

- 1/4 cup granulated sugar
- 1 teaspoon ground ginger

Instructions:

1. **Preheat Oven**: Preheat your oven to 350°F (175°C). Line a baking sheet with parchment paper or a silicone baking mat.
2. **Cream Butter and Sugars**: In a large bowl, beat the softened butter, granulated sugar, and brown sugar together until light and fluffy, about 2-3 minutes.
3. **Add Egg and Soy Sauce**: Beat in the egg and soy sauce until well combined.
4. **Mix Dry Ingredients**: In a separate bowl, whisk together the flour, ground ginger, baking soda, and salt.
5. **Combine Ingredients**: Gradually add the dry ingredients to the butter mixture, mixing until just combined.
6. **Shape the Cookies**: Roll rounded tablespoons of dough into balls and place them on the prepared baking sheet. Flatten each ball slightly with the back of a spoon.
7. **Coat with Sugar (Optional)**: If desired, mix the granulated sugar with the additional ground ginger and sprinkle it on top of the cookies before baking.
8. **Bake**: Bake in the preheated oven for 10-12 minutes, or until the edges are golden brown.
9. **Cool**: Allow the cookies to cool on the baking sheet for a few minutes before transferring them to a wire rack to cool completely.
10. **Enjoy**: Store in an airtight container for up to a week.

These Soy Sauce and Ginger Cookies offer a unique blend of sweet, savory, and spicy flavors, making them a distinctive treat that's perfect for those who enjoy exploring unconventional cookie recipes.

Azuki Bean and Sesame Cookies

Ingredients:

For the Cookies:

- 1 cup (2 sticks) unsalted butter, softened
- 1/2 cup granulated sugar
- 1/4 cup brown sugar, packed
- 1 large egg
- 1 cup cooked and mashed azuki beans (sweetened or unsweetened, depending on your preference)
- 1 3/4 cups all-purpose flour
- 1/2 teaspoon baking soda
- 1/4 teaspoon salt
- 1/4 cup toasted sesame seeds

For the Sesame Coating (Optional):

- 1/4 cup toasted sesame seeds
- 1 tablespoon granulated sugar

Instructions:

1. **Preheat Oven**: Preheat your oven to 350°F (175°C). Line a baking sheet with parchment paper or a silicone baking mat.
2. **Cream Butter and Sugars**: In a large bowl, beat the softened butter, granulated sugar, and brown sugar together until light and fluffy, about 2-3 minutes.
3. **Add Egg and Azuki Beans**: Beat in the egg until well combined. Then, mix in the mashed azuki beans.
4. **Mix Dry Ingredients**: In a separate bowl, whisk together the flour, baking soda, and salt.
5. **Combine Ingredients**: Gradually add the dry ingredients to the butter mixture, mixing until just combined. Stir in the toasted sesame seeds.
6. **Shape the Cookies**: Drop rounded tablespoons of dough onto the prepared baking sheet. Flatten each dough ball slightly with the back of a spoon.
7. **Coat with Sesame (Optional)**: Mix the additional toasted sesame seeds with granulated sugar. Sprinkle this mixture on top of each cookie before baking.
8. **Bake**: Bake in the preheated oven for 10-12 minutes, or until the edges are golden brown.
9. **Cool**: Allow the cookies to cool on the baking sheet for a few minutes before transferring them to a wire rack to cool completely.
10. **Enjoy**: Store in an airtight container for up to a week.

These Azuki Bean and Sesame Cookies offer a wonderful blend of textures and flavors, with the creamy sweetness of azuki beans complementing the crunch and nuttiness of sesame seeds. They make a unique and satisfying treat for any cookie lover.

Shiso Leaf Cookies

Ingredients:

- 1 cup (2 sticks) unsalted butter, softened
- 1/2 cup granulated sugar
- 1/4 cup powdered sugar
- 2 cups all-purpose flour
- 1/4 teaspoon salt
- 1/4 cup finely chopped fresh shiso leaves (about 10-12 leaves, or 1 tablespoon dried shiso leaves, crushed)
- Optional: 1 teaspoon vanilla extract

Instructions:

1. **Preheat Oven**: Preheat your oven to 350°F (175°C). Line a baking sheet with parchment paper or a silicone baking mat.
2. **Prepare Shiso Leaves**: If using fresh shiso leaves, finely chop them. If using dried shiso leaves, crush them into smaller pieces.
3. **Cream Butter and Sugars**: In a large bowl, beat the softened butter, granulated sugar, and powdered sugar together until light and fluffy, about 2-3 minutes.
4. **Add Vanilla (Optional)**: Mix in the vanilla extract if using.
5. **Mix Dry Ingredients**: In a separate bowl, whisk together the flour and salt.
6. **Combine Ingredients**: Gradually add the dry ingredients to the butter mixture, mixing until just combined. Stir in the chopped shiso leaves.
7. **Shape the Cookies**: Drop rounded tablespoons of dough onto the prepared baking sheet. Flatten each ball slightly with the back of a spoon or your fingers.
8. **Bake**: Bake in the preheated oven for 10-12 minutes, or until the edges are just starting to turn golden brown.
9. **Cool**: Allow the cookies to cool on the baking sheet for a few minutes before transferring them to a wire rack to cool completely.
10. **Enjoy**: Store in an airtight container for up to a week.

These Shiso Leaf Cookies have a subtly aromatic flavor that pairs beautifully with a cup of tea. The fresh or dried shiso adds a unique twist to classic cookies, making them a delightful and unexpected treat.

Sweet Potato and Cinnamon Cookies

Ingredients:

For the Cookies:

- 1 cup (2 sticks) unsalted butter, softened
- 1 cup granulated sugar
- 1/2 cup packed brown sugar
- 1 cup mashed sweet potato (about 1 medium sweet potato, cooked and mashed)
- 1 large egg
- 2 1/2 cups all-purpose flour
- 1 teaspoon ground cinnamon
- 1/2 teaspoon baking soda
- 1/2 teaspoon baking powder
- 1/4 teaspoon salt
- Optional: 1 teaspoon vanilla extract

For the Cinnamon Sugar Coating (Optional):

- 1/4 cup granulated sugar
- 1 tablespoon ground cinnamon

Instructions:

1. **Preheat Oven**: Preheat your oven to 350°F (175°C). Line a baking sheet with parchment paper or a silicone baking mat.
2. **Prepare Sweet Potato**: If you haven't already, cook and mash the sweet potato. To cook, peel and cube the sweet potato, then boil or bake until tender. Mash until smooth and let it cool to room temperature.
3. **Cream Butter and Sugars**: In a large bowl, beat the softened butter, granulated sugar, and brown sugar together until light and fluffy, about 2-3 minutes.
4. **Add Sweet Potato and Egg**: Mix in the mashed sweet potato and egg until well combined. Add vanilla extract if using.
5. **Mix Dry Ingredients**: In a separate bowl, whisk together the flour, ground cinnamon, baking soda, baking powder, and salt.
6. **Combine Ingredients**: Gradually add the dry ingredients to the butter mixture, mixing until just combined.
7. **Shape the Cookies**: Drop rounded tablespoons of dough onto the prepared baking sheet. Flatten each ball slightly with the back of a spoon.
8. **Cinnamon Sugar Coating (Optional)**: If desired, mix the granulated sugar with ground cinnamon. Sprinkle this mixture on top of each cookie before baking.
9. **Bake**: Bake in the preheated oven for 10-12 minutes, or until the edges are just starting to turn golden brown.

10. **Cool**: Allow the cookies to cool on the baking sheet for a few minutes before transferring them to a wire rack to cool completely.
11. **Enjoy**: Store in an airtight container for up to a week.

These Sweet Potato and Cinnamon Cookies have a soft, chewy texture with a wonderful blend of sweet and spicy flavors, perfect for a comforting treat!

Wasabi and White Chocolate Cookies

Ingredients:

For the Cookies:

- 1 cup (2 sticks) unsalted butter, softened
- 1/2 cup granulated sugar
- 1/4 cup brown sugar, packed
- 1 large egg
- 1 teaspoon wasabi paste (adjust to taste)
- 2 cups all-purpose flour
- 1/2 teaspoon baking soda
- 1/4 teaspoon salt
- 1 cup white chocolate chips or chunks

For the Garnish (Optional):

- 1-2 teaspoons wasabi powder (for a bit of extra heat, sprinkled on top)
- 1 tablespoon granulated sugar (for sprinkling)

Instructions:

1. **Preheat Oven**: Preheat your oven to 350°F (175°C). Line a baking sheet with parchment paper or a silicone baking mat.
2. **Cream Butter and Sugars**: In a large bowl, beat the softened butter, granulated sugar, and brown sugar together until light and fluffy, about 2-3 minutes.
3. **Add Egg and Wasabi**: Beat in the egg and wasabi paste until well combined. Adjust the amount of wasabi paste to suit your heat preference.
4. **Mix Dry Ingredients**: In a separate bowl, whisk together the flour, baking soda, and salt.
5. **Combine Ingredients**: Gradually add the dry ingredients to the butter mixture, mixing until just combined. Fold in the white chocolate chips or chunks.
6. **Shape the Cookies**: Drop rounded tablespoons of dough onto the prepared baking sheet. Flatten each ball slightly with the back of a spoon.
7. **Garnish (Optional)**: If desired, sprinkle a small pinch of wasabi powder and a little granulated sugar on top of each cookie before baking for an extra touch of flavor and visual appeal.
8. **Bake**: Bake in the preheated oven for 10-12 minutes, or until the edges are golden brown and the centers are set.
9. **Cool**: Allow the cookies to cool on the baking sheet for a few minutes before transferring them to a wire rack to cool completely.
10. **Enjoy**: Store in an airtight container for up to a week.

These Wasabi and White Chocolate Cookies provide a delightful contrast of sweet and spicy, offering a bold flavor profile that's perfect for adventurous cookie lovers!

Japanese Pumpkin Cookies

Ingredients:

For the Cookies:

- 1 cup (2 sticks) unsalted butter, softened
- 1 cup granulated sugar
- 1/2 cup packed brown sugar
- 1 cup mashed kabocha pumpkin (or other sweet pumpkin, such as butternut squash)
- 1 large egg
- 2 cups all-purpose flour
- 1 teaspoon baking soda
- 1/2 teaspoon baking powder
- 1/2 teaspoon ground cinnamon
- 1/4 teaspoon ground nutmeg
- 1/4 teaspoon ground ginger
- 1/4 teaspoon salt
- Optional: 1 teaspoon vanilla extract

For the Cinnamon Sugar Coating (Optional):

- 1/4 cup granulated sugar
- 1 teaspoon ground cinnamon

Instructions:

1. **Preheat Oven**: Preheat your oven to 350°F (175°C). Line a baking sheet with parchment paper or a silicone baking mat.
2. **Prepare Pumpkin**: If not using canned pumpkin, cook and mash the kabocha. To cook, cut the pumpkin into chunks and steam or bake until tender. Let it cool before mashing.
3. **Cream Butter and Sugars**: In a large bowl, beat the softened butter, granulated sugar, and brown sugar together until light and fluffy, about 2-3 minutes.
4. **Add Pumpkin and Egg**: Mix in the mashed pumpkin and egg until well combined. Add vanilla extract if using.
5. **Mix Dry Ingredients**: In a separate bowl, whisk together the flour, baking soda, baking powder, cinnamon, nutmeg, ginger, and salt.
6. **Combine Ingredients**: Gradually add the dry ingredients to the butter mixture, mixing until just combined.
7. **Shape the Cookies**: Drop rounded tablespoons of dough onto the prepared baking sheet. Flatten each ball slightly with the back of a spoon.
8. **Cinnamon Sugar Coating (Optional)**: If desired, mix the granulated sugar with ground cinnamon and sprinkle it on top of each cookie before baking.

9. **Bake**: Bake in the preheated oven for 10-12 minutes, or until the edges are golden brown and the centers are set.
10. **Cool**: Allow the cookies to cool on the baking sheet for a few minutes before transferring them to a wire rack to cool completely.
11. **Enjoy**: Store in an airtight container for up to a week.

These Japanese Pumpkin Cookies have a soft and tender texture with a lovely blend of spices, making them a perfect treat for autumn or anytime you want a comforting, seasonal cookie.

Umeshu (Plum Wine) Cookies

Ingredients:

For the Cookies:

- 1 cup (2 sticks) unsalted butter, softened
- 1/2 cup granulated sugar
- 1/4 cup powdered sugar
- 1/4 cup umeshu (plum wine)
- 1 large egg
- 2 cups all-purpose flour
- 1/2 teaspoon baking soda
- 1/4 teaspoon salt
- Optional: 1 teaspoon vanilla extract

For the Glaze (Optional):

- 1/2 cup powdered sugar
- 2 tablespoons umeshu (plum wine)
- Optional: Additional umeshu for brushing on the cookies

Instructions:

1. **Preheat Oven**: Preheat your oven to 350°F (175°C). Line a baking sheet with parchment paper or a silicone baking mat.
2. **Cream Butter and Sugars**: In a large bowl, beat the softened butter, granulated sugar, and powdered sugar together until light and fluffy, about 2-3 minutes.
3. **Add Egg and Umeshu**: Mix in the egg and umeshu until well combined. Add vanilla extract if using.
4. **Mix Dry Ingredients**: In a separate bowl, whisk together the flour, baking soda, and salt.
5. **Combine Ingredients**: Gradually add the dry ingredients to the butter mixture, mixing until just combined.
6. **Shape the Cookies**: Drop rounded tablespoons of dough onto the prepared baking sheet. Flatten each ball slightly with the back of a spoon or your fingers.
7. **Bake**: Bake in the preheated oven for 10-12 minutes, or until the edges are just starting to turn golden brown and the centers are set.
8. **Cool**: Allow the cookies to cool on the baking sheet for a few minutes before transferring them to a wire rack to cool completely.
9. **Prepare Glaze (Optional)**: While the cookies are cooling, whisk together the powdered sugar and umeshu until smooth. If you like, you can lightly brush additional umeshu on the cooled cookies before applying the glaze for extra flavor.
10. **Glaze the Cookies (Optional)**: Once the cookies are completely cool, drizzle or spread the glaze over the top of each cookie. Let the glaze set before storing.

11. **Enjoy**: Store in an airtight container for up to a week.

These Umeshu (Plum Wine) Cookies have a distinct plum wine flavor that adds a sophisticated twist to traditional cookies, making them a delightful treat for those who appreciate unique and elegant flavors.

Matcha Macadamia Nut Cookies

Ingredients:

For the Cookies:

- 1 cup (2 sticks) unsalted butter, softened
- 1/2 cup granulated sugar
- 1/2 cup packed brown sugar
- 1 large egg
- 2 tablespoons matcha green tea powder
- 2 cups all-purpose flour
- 1/2 teaspoon baking soda
- 1/4 teaspoon salt
- 1 cup macadamia nuts, coarsely chopped
- Optional: 1 teaspoon vanilla extract

For the Garnish (Optional):

- 1 tablespoon granulated sugar (for sprinkling)

Instructions:

1. **Preheat Oven**: Preheat your oven to 350°F (175°C). Line a baking sheet with parchment paper or a silicone baking mat.
2. **Cream Butter and Sugars**: In a large bowl, beat the softened butter, granulated sugar, and brown sugar together until light and fluffy, about 2-3 minutes.
3. **Add Egg and Matcha**: Beat in the egg until well combined. Mix in the matcha powder and vanilla extract (if using).
4. **Mix Dry Ingredients**: In a separate bowl, whisk together the flour, baking soda, and salt.
5. **Combine Ingredients**: Gradually add the dry ingredients to the butter mixture, mixing until just combined. Fold in the chopped macadamia nuts.
6. **Shape the Cookies**: Drop rounded tablespoons of dough onto the prepared baking sheet, spacing them about 2 inches apart. Flatten each ball slightly with the back of a spoon.
7. **Garnish (Optional)**: If desired, sprinkle a small amount of granulated sugar on top of each cookie for extra sweetness and a bit of sparkle.
8. **Bake**: Bake in the preheated oven for 10-12 minutes, or until the edges are just starting to turn golden brown and the centers are set.
9. **Cool**: Allow the cookies to cool on the baking sheet for a few minutes before transferring them to a wire rack to cool completely.
10. **Enjoy**: Store in an airtight container for up to a week.

These Matcha Macadamia Nut Cookies offer a delightful balance of flavors with the earthy notes of matcha complementing the rich, creamy macadamia nuts. They're a great treat for those who enjoy the unique combination of green tea and nuts!

Brown Sugar and Ginger Cookies

Ingredients:

For the Cookies:

- 1 cup (2 sticks) unsalted butter, softened
- 1 cup packed brown sugar
- 1/4 cup granulated sugar
- 1 large egg
- 1/4 cup molasses
- 2 1/4 cups all-purpose flour
- 1 teaspoon ground ginger
- 1/2 teaspoon ground cinnamon
- 1/4 teaspoon ground cloves
- 1/2 teaspoon baking soda
- 1/4 teaspoon salt

For the Sugar Coating (Optional):

- 1/4 cup granulated sugar
- 1 teaspoon ground ginger

Instructions:

1. **Preheat Oven**: Preheat your oven to 350°F (175°C). Line a baking sheet with parchment paper or a silicone baking mat.
2. **Cream Butter and Sugars**: In a large bowl, beat the softened butter, brown sugar, and granulated sugar together until light and fluffy, about 2-3 minutes.
3. **Add Egg and Molasses**: Beat in the egg and molasses until well combined.
4. **Mix Dry Ingredients**: In a separate bowl, whisk together the flour, ground ginger, ground cinnamon, ground cloves, baking soda, and salt.
5. **Combine Ingredients**: Gradually add the dry ingredients to the butter mixture, mixing until just combined.
6. **Shape the Cookies**: Drop rounded tablespoons of dough onto the prepared baking sheet. Flatten each ball slightly with the back of a spoon or your fingers.
7. **Sugar Coating (Optional)**: If desired, mix the granulated sugar with the ground ginger and sprinkle this mixture on top of each cookie before baking.
8. **Bake**: Bake in the preheated oven for 10-12 minutes, or until the edges are golden brown and the centers are set.
9. **Cool**: Allow the cookies to cool on the baking sheet for a few minutes before transferring them to a wire rack to cool completely.
10. **Enjoy**: Store in an airtight container for up to a week.

These Brown Sugar and Ginger Cookies have a perfect blend of sweet and spicy flavors, making them a comforting treat that's ideal for any time of the year. Enjoy their soft, chewy texture and warm aroma!

Black Sesame and Coconut Cookies

Ingredients:

For the Cookies:

- 1 cup (2 sticks) unsalted butter, softened
- 1 cup granulated sugar
- 1/2 cup packed brown sugar
- 1 large egg
- 1 teaspoon vanilla extract
- 1 cup shredded coconut (unsweetened or sweetened, depending on your preference)
- 1/2 cup black sesame seeds, toasted
- 2 cups all-purpose flour
- 1/2 teaspoon baking soda
- 1/4 teaspoon salt

For the Garnish (Optional):

- 1/4 cup additional black sesame seeds (for sprinkling on top)

Instructions:

1. **Preheat Oven**: Preheat your oven to 350°F (175°C). Line a baking sheet with parchment paper or a silicone baking mat.
2. **Prepare Sesame Seeds**: If your black sesame seeds are not already toasted, toast them in a dry skillet over medium heat until fragrant, about 2-3 minutes. Let them cool before using.
3. **Cream Butter and Sugars**: In a large bowl, beat the softened butter, granulated sugar, and brown sugar together until light and fluffy, about 2-3 minutes.
4. **Add Egg and Vanilla**: Mix in the egg and vanilla extract until well combined.
5. **Mix Dry Ingredients**: In a separate bowl, whisk together the flour, baking soda, and salt.
6. **Combine Ingredients**: Gradually add the dry ingredients to the butter mixture, mixing until just combined. Stir in the shredded coconut and toasted black sesame seeds.
7. **Shape the Cookies**: Drop rounded tablespoons of dough onto the prepared baking sheet. Flatten each ball slightly with the back of a spoon or your fingers.
8. **Garnish (Optional)**: If desired, sprinkle a few additional black sesame seeds on top of each cookie before baking for extra texture and visual appeal.
9. **Bake**: Bake in the preheated oven for 10-12 minutes, or until the edges are golden brown and the centers are set.
10. **Cool**: Allow the cookies to cool on the baking sheet for a few minutes before transferring them to a wire rack to cool completely.
11. **Enjoy**: Store in an airtight container for up to a week.

These Black Sesame and Coconut Cookies offer a crunchy, nutty, and slightly sweet flavor, making them a unique and enjoyable treat that pairs well with a cup of tea or coffee.

Japanese Whiskey Cookies

Ingredients:

For the Cookies:

- 1 cup (2 sticks) unsalted butter, softened
- 1/2 cup granulated sugar
- 1/2 cup packed brown sugar
- 1 large egg
- 2 tablespoons Japanese whiskey (such as Yamazaki or Hibiki)
- 2 cups all-purpose flour
- 1/2 teaspoon baking soda
- 1/4 teaspoon salt
- Optional: 1 teaspoon vanilla extract

For the Glaze (Optional):

- 1/2 cup powdered sugar
- 2 tablespoons Japanese whiskey (adjust for desired consistency)

Instructions:

1. **Preheat Oven**: Preheat your oven to 350°F (175°C). Line a baking sheet with parchment paper or a silicone baking mat.
2. **Cream Butter and Sugars**: In a large bowl, beat the softened butter, granulated sugar, and brown sugar together until light and fluffy, about 2-3 minutes.
3. **Add Egg and Whiskey**: Beat in the egg and Japanese whiskey until well combined. Add vanilla extract if using.
4. **Mix Dry Ingredients**: In a separate bowl, whisk together the flour, baking soda, and salt.
5. **Combine Ingredients**: Gradually add the dry ingredients to the butter mixture, mixing until just combined.
6. **Shape the Cookies**: Drop rounded tablespoons of dough onto the prepared baking sheet. Flatten each ball slightly with the back of a spoon or your fingers.
7. **Bake**: Bake in the preheated oven for 10-12 minutes, or until the edges are golden brown and the centers are set.
8. **Cool**: Allow the cookies to cool on the baking sheet for a few minutes before transferring them to a wire rack to cool completely.
9. **Prepare Glaze (Optional)**: While the cookies are cooling, whisk together the powdered sugar and Japanese whiskey until smooth. Adjust the amount of whiskey to achieve your desired consistency.
10. **Glaze the Cookies (Optional)**: Once the cookies are completely cool, drizzle or spread the glaze over the top of each cookie. Let the glaze set before storing.
11. **Enjoy**: Store in an airtight container for up to a week.

These Japanese Whiskey Cookies have a delicate whiskey flavor that adds sophistication to the classic cookie, making them a special treat for those who appreciate the nuanced taste of Japanese whiskey.

Honey and Soy CookiesCherry Blossom Cookies

Ingredients:

For the Cookies:

- 1 cup (2 sticks) unsalted butter, softened
- 1/2 cup granulated sugar
- 1/2 cup packed brown sugar
- 1/4 cup honey
- 1 tablespoon soy sauce
- 1 large egg
- 2 1/4 cups all-purpose flour
- 1/2 teaspoon baking soda
- 1/4 teaspoon salt

For the Garnish (Optional):

- 1 tablespoon sesame seeds or flaky sea salt

Instructions:

1. **Preheat Oven**: Preheat your oven to 350°F (175°C). Line a baking sheet with parchment paper or a silicone baking mat.
2. **Cream Butter and Sugars**: In a large bowl, beat the softened butter, granulated sugar, and brown sugar together until light and fluffy, about 2-3 minutes.
3. **Add Honey, Soy Sauce, and Egg**: Mix in the honey, soy sauce, and egg until well combined.
4. **Mix Dry Ingredients**: In a separate bowl, whisk together the flour, baking soda, and salt.
5. **Combine Ingredients**: Gradually add the dry ingredients to the butter mixture, mixing until just combined.
6. **Shape the Cookies**: Drop rounded tablespoons of dough onto the prepared baking sheet. Flatten each ball slightly with the back of a spoon or your fingers.
7. **Garnish (Optional)**: Sprinkle sesame seeds or flaky sea salt on top of each cookie before baking for added texture and flavor.
8. **Bake**: Bake in the preheated oven for 10-12 minutes, or until the edges are golden brown and the centers are set.
9. **Cool**: Allow the cookies to cool on the baking sheet for a few minutes before transferring them to a wire rack to cool completely.
10. **Enjoy**: Store in an airtight container for up to a week.

Cherry Blossom Cookies

Ingredients:

For the Cookies:

- 1 cup (2 sticks) unsalted butter, softened
- 1 cup granulated sugar
- 1 large egg
- 1 teaspoon vanilla extract
- 2 1/2 cups all-purpose flour
- 1/2 teaspoon baking powder
- 1/4 teaspoon salt
- 1-2 tablespoons cherry blossom salt or cherry blossom extract (available in specialty stores or online)

For the Glaze (Optional):

- 1/2 cup powdered sugar
- 1-2 tablespoons milk or water
- 1/2 teaspoon cherry blossom extract (for flavor)

For Decoration (Optional):

- Edible cherry blossom petals (for garnish)

Instructions:

1. **Preheat Oven**: Preheat your oven to 350°F (175°C). Line a baking sheet with parchment paper or a silicone baking mat.
2. **Cream Butter and Sugar**: In a large bowl, beat the softened butter and granulated sugar together until light and fluffy, about 2-3 minutes.
3. **Add Egg and Vanilla**: Mix in the egg and vanilla extract until well combined.
4. **Mix Dry Ingredients**: In a separate bowl, whisk together the flour, baking powder, and salt.
5. **Combine Ingredients**: Gradually add the dry ingredients to the butter mixture, mixing until just combined. Stir in the cherry blossom salt or extract.
6. **Shape the Cookies**: Drop rounded tablespoons of dough onto the prepared baking sheet. Flatten each ball slightly with the back of a spoon or your fingers.
7. **Bake**: Bake in the preheated oven for 10-12 minutes, or until the edges are just starting to turn golden brown.
8. **Cool**: Allow the cookies to cool on the baking sheet for a few minutes before transferring them to a wire rack to cool completely.

9. **Prepare Glaze (Optional)**: If using, whisk together the powdered sugar and milk or water until smooth. Stir in cherry blossom extract if desired. Drizzle over the cooled cookies.
10. **Decorate (Optional)**: Garnish with edible cherry blossom petals if using.
11. **Enjoy**: Store in an airtight container for up to a week.

Both these cookies offer a delightful twist on traditional recipes, featuring flavors that are both unique and sophisticated.

Yuzu Lemon Cookies

Ingredients:

For the Cookies:

- 1 cup (2 sticks) unsalted butter, softened
- 1 cup granulated sugar
- 1 large egg
- 2 tablespoons yuzu juice (fresh or bottled)
- 1 tablespoon lemon juice
- 1 tablespoon lemon zest
- 2 1/4 cups all-purpose flour
- 1/2 teaspoon baking powder
- 1/4 teaspoon salt
- Optional: 1 teaspoon vanilla extract

For the Glaze (Optional):

- 1 cup powdered sugar
- 2-3 tablespoons yuzu juice
- 1 tablespoon lemon juice

For Decoration (Optional):

- Lemon zest or edible flowers

Instructions:

1. **Preheat Oven**: Preheat your oven to 350°F (175°C). Line a baking sheet with parchment paper or a silicone baking mat.
2. **Cream Butter and Sugar**: In a large bowl, beat the softened butter and granulated sugar together until light and fluffy, about 2-3 minutes.
3. **Add Egg and Citrus Juices**: Mix in the egg, yuzu juice, lemon juice, and lemon zest until well combined. Add vanilla extract if using.
4. **Mix Dry Ingredients**: In a separate bowl, whisk together the flour, baking powder, and salt.
5. **Combine Ingredients**: Gradually add the dry ingredients to the butter mixture, mixing until just combined.
6. **Shape the Cookies**: Drop rounded tablespoons of dough onto the prepared baking sheet. Flatten each ball slightly with the back of a spoon or your fingers.
7. **Bake**: Bake in the preheated oven for 10-12 minutes, or until the edges are golden brown and the centers are set.

8. **Cool**: Allow the cookies to cool on the baking sheet for a few minutes before transferring them to a wire rack to cool completely.
9. **Prepare Glaze (Optional)**: While the cookies are cooling, whisk together the powdered sugar, yuzu juice, and lemon juice until smooth. Adjust the consistency with more powdered sugar or juice if needed.
10. **Glaze the Cookies (Optional)**: Once the cookies are completely cool, drizzle or spread the glaze over the top of each cookie. Let the glaze set before storing.
11. **Decorate (Optional)**: Garnish with additional lemon zest or edible flowers for a decorative touch.
12. **Enjoy**: Store in an airtight container for up to a week.

These Yuzu Lemon Cookies are bursting with citrus flavor, offering a refreshing and tangy treat that's perfect for any occasion.

Matcha and Red Bean Swirl Cookies

Ingredients:

For the Matcha Dough:

- 1 cup (2 sticks) unsalted butter, softened
- 1/2 cup granulated sugar
- 1/4 cup powdered sugar
- 1 large egg
- 2 tablespoons matcha green tea powder
- 1 3/4 cups all-purpose flour
- 1/2 teaspoon baking powder
- 1/4 teaspoon salt

For the Red Bean Swirl:

- 1/2 cup sweet red bean paste (anko), smooth or chunky as preferred

For the Egg Wash (Optional):

- 1 egg, beaten (for brushing on top)

Instructions:

1. **Preheat Oven**: Preheat your oven to 350°F (175°C). Line a baking sheet with parchment paper or a silicone baking mat.
2. **Prepare Matcha Dough**:
   - In a large bowl, cream together the softened butter, granulated sugar, and powdered sugar until light and fluffy, about 2-3 minutes.
   - Beat in the egg until well combined.
   - Sift in the matcha powder and mix until fully incorporated.
   - In a separate bowl, whisk together the flour, baking powder, and salt.
   - Gradually add the dry ingredients to the butter mixture, mixing until just combined.
3. **Prepare Red Bean Swirl**:
   - If the red bean paste is too thick, you can slightly warm it in the microwave to make it easier to spread.
4. **Assemble the Cookies**:
   - Divide the matcha dough into two equal portions.
   - Roll out one portion of the dough between two sheets of parchment paper into a rectangle (about 1/4-inch thick).
   - Spread the red bean paste evenly over the rolled-out dough.
   - Roll up the dough tightly, like a jelly roll, using the parchment paper to help.

- Repeat the process with the second portion of dough and place it on top of the red bean paste layer, pressing gently to adhere.
- Chill the rolled dough in the refrigerator for about 30 minutes to firm up.

5. **Slice and Bake**:
    - After chilling, slice the dough into 1/4-inch thick rounds.
    - Place the slices onto the prepared baking sheet, spacing them about 1-2 inches apart.
    - If using, brush the tops of the cookies with the beaten egg for a shiny finish.
6. **Bake**: Bake in the preheated oven for 10-12 minutes, or until the edges are just starting to turn golden brown.
7. **Cool**: Allow the cookies to cool on the baking sheet for a few minutes before transferring them to a wire rack to cool completely.
8. **Enjoy**: Store in an airtight container for up to a week.

These Matcha and Red Bean Swirl Cookies have a beautiful swirl pattern and a delightful combination of flavors, making them a special treat for those who appreciate the unique tastes of matcha and red bean paste.

Daifuku Mochi Cookies

Ingredients:

For the Mochi Filling:

- 1 cup sweet rice flour (mochi flour)
- 1/2 cup granulated sugar
- 1 cup water
- Cornstarch or potato starch (for dusting)

For the Cookie Dough:

- 1 cup (2 sticks) unsalted butter, softened
- 1 cup granulated sugar
- 1/2 cup packed brown sugar
- 1 large egg
- 1 teaspoon vanilla extract
- 2 1/4 cups all-purpose flour
- 1/2 teaspoon baking powder
- 1/4 teaspoon salt

For Assembly:

- Additional cornstarch or potato starch (for dusting)
- Optional: Sweet red bean paste or chocolate chips for filling

Instructions:

1. **Prepare the Mochi Filling**:
   - In a heatproof bowl, mix the sweet rice flour and granulated sugar.
   - Gradually add the water, stirring until smooth.
   - Steam the mixture in a steamer or on a heatproof plate over simmering water for about 20-25 minutes, or until the mixture is thick and translucent.
   - Allow the mochi to cool slightly, then dust your hands and work surface with cornstarch or potato starch.
   - Turn the mochi out onto the dusted surface and knead until smooth. Divide into small pieces (about 1 teaspoon each). You can also add a small dollop of sweet red bean paste or a chocolate chip to each piece if desired. Roll them into balls and set aside.
2. **Prepare the Cookie Dough**:
   - In a large bowl, beat the softened butter, granulated sugar, and brown sugar together until light and fluffy, about 2-3 minutes.
   - Beat in the egg and vanilla extract until well combined.

- In a separate bowl, whisk together the flour, baking powder, and salt.
- Gradually add the dry ingredients to the butter mixture, mixing until just combined.

3. **Assemble the Cookies**:
    - Preheat your oven to 350°F (175°C). Line a baking sheet with parchment paper or a silicone baking mat.
    - Scoop out a tablespoon of cookie dough and flatten it slightly in your hand. Place a piece of mochi in the center of the dough and wrap the dough around the mochi, sealing the edges completely.
    - Roll the filled dough ball into a smooth ball and place it on the prepared baking sheet. Flatten slightly with your hand or the bottom of a glass.

4. **Bake**:
    - Bake in the preheated oven for 10-12 minutes, or until the cookies are just starting to turn golden brown around the edges.

5. **Cool**:
    - Allow the cookies to cool on the baking sheet for a few minutes before transferring them to a wire rack to cool completely.

6. **Enjoy**:
    - Store in an airtight container for up to a week. The cookies are best enjoyed within a few days of baking, as the mochi can become firmer over time.

These Daifuku Mochi Cookies offer a delightful combination of chewy mochi filling and buttery cookie dough, providing a unique texture and flavor that's both comforting and satisfying.

Tofu and Green Tea Cookies

Ingredients:

For the Cookies:

- 1/2 cup (1 stick) unsalted butter, softened
- 1/2 cup granulated sugar
- 1/4 cup brown sugar, packed
- 1/2 cup silken tofu, drained and mashed
- 1 tablespoon matcha green tea powder
- 1 large egg
- 1 teaspoon vanilla extract
- 1 3/4 cups all-purpose flour
- 1/2 teaspoon baking powder
- 1/4 teaspoon salt

For the Garnish (Optional):

- 1 tablespoon granulated sugar (for sprinkling)
- Extra matcha powder (for dusting)

Instructions:

1. **Preheat Oven**: Preheat your oven to 350°F (175°C). Line a baking sheet with parchment paper or a silicone baking mat.
2. **Prepare Tofu**: In a bowl, mash the silken tofu until smooth. You can use a fork or an immersion blender for a smoother texture.
3. **Cream Butter and Sugars**: In a large bowl, beat the softened butter, granulated sugar, and brown sugar together until light and fluffy, about 2-3 minutes.
4. **Add Tofu and Flavorings**: Mix in the mashed tofu, matcha powder, egg, and vanilla extract until well combined.
5. **Mix Dry Ingredients**: In a separate bowl, whisk together the flour, baking powder, and salt.
6. **Combine Ingredients**: Gradually add the dry ingredients to the wet ingredients, mixing until just combined.
7. **Shape the Cookies**: Drop rounded tablespoons of dough onto the prepared baking sheet. Flatten each ball slightly with the back of a spoon or your fingers.
8. **Garnish (Optional)**: If desired, sprinkle a small amount of granulated sugar on top of each cookie and a dusting of extra matcha powder for added flavor and visual appeal.
9. **Bake**: Bake in the preheated oven for 10-12 minutes, or until the edges are golden brown and the centers are set.
10. **Cool**: Allow the cookies to cool on the baking sheet for a few minutes before transferring them to a wire rack to cool completely.

11. **Enjoy**: Store in an airtight container for up to a week.

These Tofu and Green Tea Cookies are a unique treat with a delicate green tea flavor and a tender, chewy texture from the tofu. They're perfect for those who appreciate a more subtle and nuanced cookie experience.

Takoyaki (Octopus Ball) Cookies

Ingredients:

For the Cookies:

- 1 cup (2 sticks) unsalted butter, softened
- 1/2 cup granulated sugar
- 1/2 cup packed brown sugar
- 1 large egg
- 2 tablespoons soy sauce
- 1 tablespoon mirin (sweet rice wine)
- 1 teaspoon grated ginger
- 1 3/4 cups all-purpose flour
- 1/2 teaspoon baking powder
- 1/4 teaspoon salt
- 1/4 cup bonito flakes (dried fish flakes)
- Optional: 1/4 cup finely chopped green onions (for garnish)

For the Glaze (Optional):

- 1/2 cup powdered sugar
- 1 tablespoon soy sauce
- 1-2 tablespoons water (to achieve the desired consistency)

Instructions:

1. **Preheat Oven**: Preheat your oven to 350°F (175°C). Line a baking sheet with parchment paper or a silicone baking mat.
2. **Cream Butter and Sugars**: In a large bowl, beat the softened butter, granulated sugar, and brown sugar together until light and fluffy, about 2-3 minutes.
3. **Add Egg and Flavors**: Beat in the egg, soy sauce, mirin, and grated ginger until well combined.
4. **Mix Dry Ingredients**: In a separate bowl, whisk together the flour, baking powder, and salt.
5. **Combine Ingredients**: Gradually add the dry ingredients to the butter mixture, mixing until just combined. Stir in the bonito flakes and optional green onions if using.
6. **Shape the Cookies**: Drop rounded tablespoons of dough onto the prepared baking sheet. Flatten each ball slightly with the back of a spoon or your fingers.
7. **Bake**: Bake in the preheated oven for 10-12 minutes, or until the edges are golden brown and the centers are set.
8. **Cool**: Allow the cookies to cool on the baking sheet for a few minutes before transferring them to a wire rack to cool completely.

9. **Prepare Glaze (Optional)**: If using, whisk together the powdered sugar, soy sauce, and water until smooth. Adjust the consistency with more powdered sugar or water if needed.
10. **Glaze the Cookies (Optional)**: Once the cookies are completely cool, drizzle or spread the glaze over the top of each cookie.
11. **Enjoy**: Store in an airtight container for up to a week.

These Takoyaki (Octopus Ball) Cookies offer a fun and inventive twist on traditional cookies by incorporating savory flavors inspired by takoyaki. They provide a unique tasting experience that blends sweet and savory in a playful way.

Soba Noodle Cookies

Ingredients:

For the Cookies:

- 1 cup (2 sticks) unsalted butter, softened
- 1 cup granulated sugar
- 1/2 cup packed brown sugar
- 1 large egg
- 1 teaspoon vanilla extract
- 2 cups all-purpose flour
- 1/2 teaspoon baking soda
- 1/4 teaspoon salt
- 1 cup cooked and cooled soba noodles (drained and pat dry)
- Optional: 1/2 cup chopped nuts (such as almonds or walnuts) for added texture

For the Garnish (Optional):

- 2 tablespoons sesame seeds (for sprinkling)

Instructions:

1. **Preheat Oven**: Preheat your oven to 350°F (175°C). Line a baking sheet with parchment paper or a silicone baking mat.
2. **Cook Soba Noodles**: Cook soba noodles according to package instructions, then drain and rinse under cold water. Pat the noodles dry with a paper towel to remove excess moisture. Chop the noodles into smaller pieces if they are long.
3. **Cream Butter and Sugars**: In a large bowl, beat the softened butter, granulated sugar, and brown sugar together until light and fluffy, about 2-3 minutes.
4. **Add Egg and Vanilla**: Mix in the egg and vanilla extract until well combined.
5. **Mix Dry Ingredients**: In a separate bowl, whisk together the flour, baking soda, and salt.
6. **Combine Ingredients**: Gradually add the dry ingredients to the butter mixture, mixing until just combined. Stir in the cooked soba noodles and chopped nuts if using.
7. **Shape the Cookies**: Drop rounded tablespoons of dough onto the prepared baking sheet. Flatten each ball slightly with the back of a spoon or your fingers.
8. **Garnish (Optional)**: Sprinkle sesame seeds on top of each cookie before baking for added flavor and texture.
9. **Bake**: Bake in the preheated oven for 12-15 minutes, or until the edges are golden brown and the centers are set.
10. **Cool**: Allow the cookies to cool on the baking sheet for a few minutes before transferring them to a wire rack to cool completely.
11. **Enjoy**: Store in an airtight container for up to a week.

These Soba Noodle Cookies offer a unique blend of textures, combining the crunchiness of cookies with the subtle chewiness and nutty flavor of soba noodles. The optional nuts and sesame seeds add extra flavor and texture, making these cookies a fun and inventive treat.

Taro and Coconut Cookies

Ingredients:

For the Cookies:

- 1 cup (2 sticks) unsalted butter, softened
- 1 cup granulated sugar
- 1/2 cup packed brown sugar
- 1 large egg
- 1 teaspoon vanilla extract
- 1 cup taro paste (canned or homemade, see notes)
- 2 cups all-purpose flour
- 1/2 teaspoon baking powder
- 1/4 teaspoon salt
- 1/2 cup shredded coconut (sweetened or unsweetened)

For the Garnish (Optional):

- Additional shredded coconut for sprinkling

Instructions:

1. **Preheat Oven**: Preheat your oven to 350°F (175°C). Line a baking sheet with parchment paper or a silicone baking mat.
2. **Prepare Taro Paste**: If using canned taro paste, ensure it's smooth. If using fresh taro, steam or boil taro root until tender, then mash or blend until smooth.
3. **Cream Butter and Sugars**: In a large bowl, beat the softened butter, granulated sugar, and brown sugar together until light and fluffy, about 2-3 minutes.
4. **Add Egg, Vanilla, and Taro Paste**: Mix in the egg, vanilla extract, and taro paste until well combined.
5. **Mix Dry Ingredients**: In a separate bowl, whisk together the flour, baking powder, and salt.
6. **Combine Ingredients**: Gradually add the dry ingredients to the butter mixture, mixing until just combined. Fold in the shredded coconut.
7. **Shape the Cookies**: Drop rounded tablespoons of dough onto the prepared baking sheet. Flatten each ball slightly with the back of a spoon or your fingers.
8. **Garnish (Optional)**: If desired, sprinkle additional shredded coconut on top of each cookie before baking.
9. **Bake**: Bake in the preheated oven for 12-15 minutes, or until the edges are golden brown and the centers are set.
10. **Cool**: Allow the cookies to cool on the baking sheet for a few minutes before transferring them to a wire rack to cool completely.
11. **Enjoy**: Store in an airtight container for up to a week.

Notes:

- **Taro Paste**: If you can't find canned taro paste, you can make your own by steaming or boiling taro root until soft, then mashing or blending it into a smooth paste. Ensure it's cooled before using it in the recipe.
- **Shredded Coconut**: You can use sweetened or unsweetened shredded coconut based on your preference.

These Taro and Coconut Cookies offer a delightful combination of flavors and textures, making them a unique and tasty treat for any occasion.

Almond and Uji Matcha Cookies

Ingredients:

For the Cookies:

- 1 cup (2 sticks) unsalted butter, softened
- 1 cup granulated sugar
- 1/2 cup packed brown sugar
- 1 large egg
- 1 teaspoon vanilla extract
- 2 tablespoons Uji matcha powder (or high-quality matcha)
- 1 3/4 cups all-purpose flour
- 1/2 teaspoon baking powder
- 1/4 teaspoon salt
- 1/2 cup finely chopped almonds (toasted or raw, as preferred)

For the Garnish (Optional):

- Additional granulated sugar or coarse sugar for sprinkling
- Whole almonds or sliced almonds for topping

Instructions:

1. **Preheat Oven**: Preheat your oven to 350°F (175°C). Line a baking sheet with parchment paper or a silicone baking mat.
2. **Prepare Almonds**: If using raw almonds, toast them in a dry skillet over medium heat until fragrant and lightly browned, about 5 minutes. Let cool and then finely chop.
3. **Cream Butter and Sugars**: In a large bowl, beat the softened butter, granulated sugar, and brown sugar together until light and fluffy, about 2-3 minutes.
4. **Add Egg, Vanilla, and Matcha**: Mix in the egg, vanilla extract, and Uji matcha powder until well combined.
5. **Mix Dry Ingredients**: In a separate bowl, whisk together the flour, baking powder, and salt.
6. **Combine Ingredients**: Gradually add the dry ingredients to the butter mixture, mixing until just combined. Fold in the finely chopped almonds.
7. **Shape the Cookies**: Drop rounded tablespoons of dough onto the prepared baking sheet. Flatten each ball slightly with the back of a spoon or your fingers.
8. **Garnish (Optional)**: If desired, sprinkle a small amount of granulated sugar or coarse sugar on top of each cookie and press a whole almond or a few sliced almonds into the center of each cookie.
9. **Bake**: Bake in the preheated oven for 10-12 minutes, or until the edges are golden brown and the centers are set.

10. **Cool**: Allow the cookies to cool on the baking sheet for a few minutes before transferring them to a wire rack to cool completely.
11. **Enjoy**: Store in an airtight container for up to a week.

Notes:

- **Uji Matcha**: Uji matcha is known for its high quality and vibrant color. If it's not available, any high-quality matcha powder will work, but the flavor may vary slightly.
- **Almonds**: Toasting the almonds enhances their flavor, but you can use raw almonds if you prefer a milder taste.

These Almond and Uji Matcha Cookies offer a delightful combination of nutty and earthy flavors, with a beautiful green hue from the matcha. They make a sophisticated treat that's perfect for any occasion.

Kinako (Roasted Soybean Flour) Cookies

Ingredients:

For the Cookies:

- 1 cup (2 sticks) unsalted butter, softened
- 1 cup granulated sugar
- 1/2 cup packed brown sugar
- 1 large egg
- 1 teaspoon vanilla extract
- 1/2 cup kinako (roasted soybean flour)
- 1 1/2 cups all-purpose flour
- 1/2 teaspoon baking powder
- 1/4 teaspoon salt

For the Garnish (Optional):

- Extra kinako for dusting
- Optional: 1/4 cup white chocolate chips or chopped nuts for added texture

Instructions:

1. **Preheat Oven**: Preheat your oven to 350°F (175°C). Line a baking sheet with parchment paper or a silicone baking mat.
2. **Cream Butter and Sugars**: In a large bowl, beat the softened butter, granulated sugar, and brown sugar together until light and fluffy, about 2-3 minutes.
3. **Add Egg and Vanilla**: Mix in the egg and vanilla extract until well combined.
4. **Add Kinako**: Stir in the kinako until well incorporated.
5. **Mix Dry Ingredients**: In a separate bowl, whisk together the flour, baking powder, and salt.
6. **Combine Ingredients**: Gradually add the dry ingredients to the butter mixture, mixing until just combined. If using, fold in the white chocolate chips or chopped nuts at this stage.
7. **Shape the Cookies**: Drop rounded tablespoons of dough onto the prepared baking sheet. Flatten each ball slightly with the back of a spoon or your fingers.
8. **Garnish (Optional)**: If desired, lightly dust the tops of the cookies with extra kinako before baking for added flavor.
9. **Bake**: Bake in the preheated oven for 10-12 minutes, or until the edges are golden brown and the centers are set.
10. **Cool**: Allow the cookies to cool on the baking sheet for a few minutes before transferring them to a wire rack to cool completely.
11. **Enjoy**: Store in an airtight container for up to a week.

Notes:

- **Kinako**: Kinako is available in Asian grocery stores or online. It adds a unique roasted, nutty flavor to the cookies, which is a distinctive characteristic of these treats.
- **Texture Variations**: You can add white chocolate chips or chopped nuts to enhance the texture and flavor of the cookies, but they are optional.

These Kinako Cookies offer a delightful blend of nutty and sweet flavors, with a distinct roasted soybean taste that sets them apart from traditional cookies. They are perfect for anyone looking to try a unique and flavorful cookie.

Yatsuhashi (Sweet Rice Flour) Cookies

Ingredients:

For the Cookies:

- 1 cup (2 sticks) unsalted butter, softened
- 1 cup granulated sugar
- 1/2 cup packed brown sugar
- 1 large egg
- 1 teaspoon vanilla extract
- 1/2 cup sweet rice flour (mochi flour)
- 1 1/2 cups all-purpose flour
- 1/2 teaspoon baking powder
- 1/4 teaspoon salt

For the Cinnamon Sugar Coating (Optional):

- 1/4 cup granulated sugar
- 1 teaspoon ground cinnamon

Instructions:

1. **Preheat Oven**: Preheat your oven to 350°F (175°C). Line a baking sheet with parchment paper or a silicone baking mat.
2. **Cream Butter and Sugars**: In a large bowl, beat the softened butter, granulated sugar, and brown sugar together until light and fluffy, about 2-3 minutes.
3. **Add Egg and Vanilla**: Mix in the egg and vanilla extract until well combined.
4. **Add Sweet Rice Flour**: Stir in the sweet rice flour until well incorporated.
5. **Mix Dry Ingredients**: In a separate bowl, whisk together the all-purpose flour, baking powder, and salt.
6. **Combine Ingredients**: Gradually add the dry ingredients to the butter mixture, mixing until just combined.
7. **Shape the Cookies**: Drop rounded tablespoons of dough onto the prepared baking sheet. Flatten each ball slightly with the back of a spoon or your fingers.
8. **Optional Coating**: If using the cinnamon sugar coating, mix the granulated sugar and ground cinnamon in a small bowl. Roll each cookie dough ball in the cinnamon sugar mixture before placing them on the baking sheet.
9. **Bake**: Bake in the preheated oven for 10-12 minutes, or until the edges are golden brown and the centers are set.
10. **Cool**: Allow the cookies to cool on the baking sheet for a few minutes before transferring them to a wire rack to cool completely.
11. **Enjoy**: Store in an airtight container for up to a week.

Notes:

- **Sweet Rice Flour**: Sweet rice flour, or mochiko, is different from regular rice flour. It gives the cookies a chewy texture that resembles traditional Yatsuhashi sweets.
- **Texture**: The cookies will have a slightly chewy interior thanks to the sweet rice flour, with a crisp exterior if baked until golden.

These Yatsuhashi Cookies offer a unique twist on traditional cookies, incorporating the chewy texture of sweet rice flour for a delightful Japanese-inspired treat.

Ginger and Soy Cookies

Ingredients:

For the Cookies:

- 1 cup (2 sticks) unsalted butter, softened
- 1 cup granulated sugar
- 1/2 cup packed brown sugar
- 1 large egg
- 1 tablespoon soy sauce
- 2 teaspoons ground ginger
- 1 3/4 cups all-purpose flour
- 1/2 teaspoon baking powder
- 1/4 teaspoon baking soda
- 1/4 teaspoon salt

For the Garnish (Optional):

- 1 tablespoon granulated sugar (for sprinkling)
- 1/2 teaspoon ground ginger (for sprinkling)

Instructions:

1. **Preheat Oven**: Preheat your oven to 350°F (175°C). Line a baking sheet with parchment paper or a silicone baking mat.
2. **Cream Butter and Sugars**: In a large bowl, beat the softened butter, granulated sugar, and brown sugar together until light and fluffy, about 2-3 minutes.
3. **Add Egg, Soy Sauce, and Ginger**: Mix in the egg, soy sauce, and ground ginger until well combined.
4. **Mix Dry Ingredients**: In a separate bowl, whisk together the flour, baking powder, baking soda, and salt.
5. **Combine Ingredients**: Gradually add the dry ingredients to the butter mixture, mixing until just combined.
6. **Shape the Cookies**: Drop rounded tablespoons of dough onto the prepared baking sheet. Flatten each ball slightly with the back of a spoon or your fingers.
7. **Garnish (Optional)**: If desired, sprinkle a small amount of granulated sugar and a pinch of ground ginger on top of each cookie before baking.
8. **Bake**: Bake in the preheated oven for 10-12 minutes, or until the edges are golden brown and the centers are set.
9. **Cool**: Allow the cookies to cool on the baking sheet for a few minutes before transferring them to a wire rack to cool completely.
10. **Enjoy**: Store in an airtight container for up to a week.

Notes:

- **Soy Sauce**: The soy sauce adds a unique umami depth to the cookies, complementing the spicy ginger flavor. Use a light soy sauce for a milder taste.
- **Texture**: The cookies will have a slightly chewy interior with a crisp exterior, enhanced by the savory soy sauce and spicy ginger.

These Ginger and Soy Cookies offer an innovative blend of flavors, perfect for those looking to try something different from traditional cookie recipes. Enjoy these cookies with a cup of tea or as a unique treat for special occasions!

Sweet Red Bean and Matcha Cookies

Ingredients:

For the Cookies:

- 1 cup (2 sticks) unsalted butter, softened
- 1 cup granulated sugar
- 1/2 cup packed brown sugar
- 1 large egg
- 1 teaspoon vanilla extract
- 2 tablespoons matcha powder (high-quality preferred)
- 1 3/4 cups all-purpose flour
- 1/2 teaspoon baking powder
- 1/4 teaspoon salt
- 1/2 cup sweet red bean paste (anko, smooth or chunky)

For the Garnish (Optional):

- Extra matcha powder for dusting
- Additional granulated sugar for sprinkling

Instructions:

1. **Preheat Oven**: Preheat your oven to 350°F (175°C). Line a baking sheet with parchment paper or a silicone baking mat.
2. **Cream Butter and Sugars**: In a large bowl, beat the softened butter, granulated sugar, and brown sugar together until light and fluffy, about 2-3 minutes.
3. **Add Egg and Vanilla**: Mix in the egg and vanilla extract until well combined.
4. **Incorporate Matcha**: Stir in the matcha powder until fully combined.
5. **Mix Dry Ingredients**: In a separate bowl, whisk together the flour, baking powder, and salt.
6. **Combine Ingredients**: Gradually add the dry ingredients to the butter mixture, mixing until just combined.
7. **Add Red Bean Paste**: Gently fold in the sweet red bean paste. The red bean paste may create swirls or lumps in the dough, which is okay.
8. **Shape the Cookies**: Drop rounded tablespoons of dough onto the prepared baking sheet. Flatten each ball slightly with the back of a spoon or your fingers. You can also use a cookie scoop for uniform shapes.
9. **Garnish (Optional)**: If desired, sprinkle a small amount of granulated sugar on top of each cookie and lightly dust with extra matcha powder.
10. **Bake**: Bake in the preheated oven for 12-15 minutes, or until the edges are golden brown and the centers are set.

11. **Cool**: Allow the cookies to cool on the baking sheet for a few minutes before transferring them to a wire rack to cool completely.
12. **Enjoy**: Store in an airtight container for up to a week.

Notes:

- **Sweet Red Bean Paste**: Sweet red bean paste (anko) is available at Asian grocery stores. If using homemade, ensure it is smooth and not too runny. If using chunky, it may add interesting texture to the cookies.
- **Matcha Powder**: High-quality matcha powder will provide the best flavor and vibrant green color.

These Sweet Red Bean and Matcha Cookies combine the rich flavors of matcha and sweet red beans for a unique and delightful treat. They make a perfect addition to tea time or as a special treat for any occasion.

Kabocha (Japanese Pumpkin) and Spice Cookies

Ingredients:

For the Cookies:

- 1 cup (2 sticks) unsalted butter, softened
- 1 cup granulated sugar
- 1/2 cup packed brown sugar
- 1 large egg
- 1 cup kabocha puree (see notes for how to prepare)
- 1 teaspoon vanilla extract
- 2 1/4 cups all-purpose flour
- 1/2 teaspoon baking powder
- 1/2 teaspoon baking soda
- 1/4 teaspoon salt
- 1 teaspoon ground cinnamon
- 1/2 teaspoon ground nutmeg
- 1/4 teaspoon ground cloves
- 1/4 teaspoon ground ginger

For the Garnish (Optional):

- 1/4 cup granulated sugar (for sprinkling)
- 1/2 teaspoon ground cinnamon (for sprinkling)

Instructions:

1. **Preheat Oven**: Preheat your oven to 350°F (175°C). Line a baking sheet with parchment paper or a silicone baking mat.
2. **Prepare Kabocha Puree**: If using fresh kabocha, cut it into pieces, remove the seeds, and roast or steam until tender. Scoop the flesh into a blender or food processor and blend until smooth. Let it cool before using. You can also use canned kabocha or pumpkin puree if fresh is not available.
3. **Cream Butter and Sugars**: In a large bowl, beat the softened butter, granulated sugar, and brown sugar together until light and fluffy, about 2-3 minutes.
4. **Add Egg, Kabocha Puree, and Vanilla**: Mix in the egg, kabocha puree, and vanilla extract until well combined.
5. **Mix Dry Ingredients**: In a separate bowl, whisk together the flour, baking powder, baking soda, salt, cinnamon, nutmeg, cloves, and ginger.
6. **Combine Ingredients**: Gradually add the dry ingredients to the butter mixture, mixing until just combined.
7. **Shape the Cookies**: Drop rounded tablespoons of dough onto the prepared baking sheet. Flatten each ball slightly with the back of a spoon or your fingers.

8. **Garnish (Optional)**: If desired, sprinkle a small amount of granulated sugar and ground cinnamon on top of each cookie before baking.
9. **Bake**: Bake in the preheated oven for 12-15 minutes, or until the edges are golden brown and the centers are set.
10. **Cool**: Allow the cookies to cool on the baking sheet for a few minutes before transferring them to a wire rack to cool completely.
11. **Enjoy**: Store in an airtight container for up to a week.

Notes:

- **Kabocha Puree**: If you can't find kabocha, you can substitute with canned pumpkin puree. Ensure it's not pumpkin pie filling, which contains added spices and sugar.
- **Spices**: Adjust the spices to your taste. For a more intense flavor, you can increase the amounts slightly or add a pinch of allspice.

These Kabocha and Spice Cookies are warm and comforting, with the rich flavor of Japanese pumpkin and aromatic spices. They're perfect for fall or whenever you're in the mood for a cozy, flavorful cookie.

Yuzu and Sesame Cookies

Ingredients:

For the Cookies:

- 1 cup (2 sticks) unsalted butter, softened
- 1 cup granulated sugar
- 1/2 cup packed brown sugar
- 1 large egg
- 2 tablespoons yuzu juice (fresh or bottled, see notes)
- 1 teaspoon yuzu zest (optional, for extra flavor)
- 2 cups all-purpose flour
- 1/2 teaspoon baking powder
- 1/4 teaspoon salt
- 1/2 cup toasted sesame seeds (white or black)

For the Garnish (Optional):

- Extra sesame seeds for sprinkling

Instructions:

1. **Preheat Oven**: Preheat your oven to 350°F (175°C). Line a baking sheet with parchment paper or a silicone baking mat.
2. **Cream Butter and Sugars**: In a large bowl, beat the softened butter, granulated sugar, and brown sugar together until light and fluffy, about 2-3 minutes.
3. **Add Egg, Yuzu Juice, and Zest**: Mix in the egg, yuzu juice, and yuzu zest (if using) until well combined.
4. **Mix Dry Ingredients**: In a separate bowl, whisk together the flour, baking powder, and salt.
5. **Combine Ingredients**: Gradually add the dry ingredients to the butter mixture, mixing until just combined. Fold in the toasted sesame seeds.
6. **Shape the Cookies**: Drop rounded tablespoons of dough onto the prepared baking sheet. Flatten each ball slightly with the back of a spoon or your fingers.
7. **Garnish (Optional)**: If desired, sprinkle additional sesame seeds on top of each cookie before baking.
8. **Bake**: Bake in the preheated oven for 10-12 minutes, or until the edges are golden brown and the centers are set.
9. **Cool**: Allow the cookies to cool on the baking sheet for a few minutes before transferring them to a wire rack to cool completely.
10. **Enjoy**: Store in an airtight container for up to a week.

Notes:

- **Yuzu Juice**: Yuzu juice can be found in Asian grocery stores or online. If fresh yuzu is unavailable, bottled yuzu juice is a good substitute. Adjust the amount of juice to taste, as it can vary in intensity.
- **Toasted Sesame Seeds**: Toasted sesame seeds add a nutty flavor and crunch. You can toast them in a dry skillet over medium heat until they become fragrant, about 3-5 minutes.

These Yuzu and Sesame Cookies are a delightful combination of citrusy brightness and nutty richness, perfect for a unique and refreshing treat. Enjoy these cookies with a cup of tea or as a special dessert!

Maple and Azuki Cookies

Ingredients:

For the Cookies:

- 1 cup (2 sticks) unsalted butter, softened
- 1 cup granulated sugar
- 1/2 cup packed brown sugar
- 1/2 cup pure maple syrup
- 1 large egg
- 1 teaspoon vanilla extract
- 2 cups all-purpose flour
- 1/2 teaspoon baking powder
- 1/4 teaspoon salt
- 1/2 cup sweet red bean paste (anko, smooth or chunky, see notes)

For the Garnish (Optional):

- 1/4 cup granulated sugar (for sprinkling)

Instructions:

1. **Preheat Oven**: Preheat your oven to 350°F (175°C). Line a baking sheet with parchment paper or a silicone baking mat.
2. **Cream Butter and Sugars**: In a large bowl, beat the softened butter, granulated sugar, and brown sugar together until light and fluffy, about 2-3 minutes.
3. **Add Maple Syrup, Egg, and Vanilla**: Mix in the maple syrup, egg, and vanilla extract until well combined.
4. **Mix Dry Ingredients**: In a separate bowl, whisk together the flour, baking powder, and salt.
5. **Combine Ingredients**: Gradually add the dry ingredients to the butter mixture, mixing until just combined. Gently fold in the sweet red bean paste. If the paste is chunky, it will create interesting textures in the cookies.
6. **Shape the Cookies**: Drop rounded tablespoons of dough onto the prepared baking sheet. Flatten each ball slightly with the back of a spoon or your fingers.
7. **Garnish (Optional)**: If desired, sprinkle a small amount of granulated sugar on top of each cookie before baking.
8. **Bake**: Bake in the preheated oven for 12-15 minutes, or until the edges are golden brown and the centers are set.
9. **Cool**: Allow the cookies to cool on the baking sheet for a few minutes before transferring them to a wire rack to cool completely.
10. **Enjoy**: Store in an airtight container for up to a week.

Notes:

- **Sweet Red Bean Paste**: Sweet red bean paste (anko) can be found at Asian grocery stores. If using homemade, ensure it is smooth and not too runny. If using chunky paste, it will add texture to the cookies.
- **Maple Syrup**: Use pure maple syrup for the best flavor. Avoid imitation maple syrup as it has a different taste.

These Maple and Azuki Cookies offer a delightful combination of sweet maple syrup and the rich, nutty flavor of azuki beans. They make a wonderful treat for any occasion, with a unique twist that will impress your family and friends.

Black Sugar Cookies

Ingredients:

For the Cookies:

- 1 cup (2 sticks) unsalted butter, softened
- 1 cup black sugar (kokuto) or dark brown sugar
- 1/2 cup granulated sugar
- 1 large egg
- 1 teaspoon vanilla extract
- 2 1/4 cups all-purpose flour
- 1/2 teaspoon baking powder
- 1/4 teaspoon baking soda
- 1/4 teaspoon salt

For the Garnish (Optional):

- Extra black sugar or granulated sugar for sprinkling

Instructions:

1. **Preheat Oven**: Preheat your oven to 350°F (175°C). Line a baking sheet with parchment paper or a silicone baking mat.
2. **Cream Butter and Sugars**: In a large bowl, beat the softened butter, black sugar, and granulated sugar together until light and fluffy, about 2-3 minutes.
3. **Add Egg and Vanilla**: Mix in the egg and vanilla extract until well combined.
4. **Mix Dry Ingredients**: In a separate bowl, whisk together the flour, baking powder, baking soda, and salt.
5. **Combine Ingredients**: Gradually add the dry ingredients to the butter mixture, mixing until just combined.
6. **Shape the Cookies**: Drop rounded tablespoons of dough onto the prepared baking sheet. Flatten each ball slightly with the back of a spoon or your fingers.
7. **Garnish (Optional)**: If desired, sprinkle a small amount of black sugar or granulated sugar on top of each cookie before baking.
8. **Bake**: Bake in the preheated oven for 10-12 minutes, or until the edges are golden brown and the centers are set.
9. **Cool**: Allow the cookies to cool on the baking sheet for a few minutes before transferring them to a wire rack to cool completely.
10. **Enjoy**: Store in an airtight container for up to a week.

Notes:

- **Black Sugar**: Black sugar, also known as kokuto, is available at Asian grocery stores or online. If you can't find black sugar, dark brown sugar is a good substitute, though the flavor will be slightly different.
- **Texture**: These cookies will have a slightly chewy texture with a rich, caramel flavor due to the black sugar.

These Black Sugar Cookies offer a unique and delicious twist on classic cookies, with the deep, molasses-like sweetness of black sugar. Enjoy them with a cup of tea or as a special treat!

Matcha and White Sesame Cookies

Ingredients:

For the Cookies:

- 1 cup (2 sticks) unsalted butter, softened
- 1 cup granulated sugar
- 1/2 cup packed brown sugar
- 1 large egg
- 1 teaspoon vanilla extract
- 2 tablespoons matcha powder (high-quality preferred)
- 1 3/4 cups all-purpose flour
- 1/2 teaspoon baking powder
- 1/4 teaspoon baking soda
- 1/4 teaspoon salt
- 1/2 cup white sesame seeds (toasted if preferred)

For the Garnish (Optional):

- Extra white sesame seeds for sprinkling

Instructions:

1. **Preheat Oven**: Preheat your oven to 350°F (175°C). Line a baking sheet with parchment paper or a silicone baking mat.
2. **Cream Butter and Sugars**: In a large bowl, beat the softened butter, granulated sugar, and brown sugar together until light and fluffy, about 2-3 minutes.
3. **Add Egg, Vanilla, and Matcha**: Mix in the egg, vanilla extract, and matcha powder until well combined.
4. **Mix Dry Ingredients**: In a separate bowl, whisk together the flour, baking powder, baking soda, and salt.
5. **Combine Ingredients**: Gradually add the dry ingredients to the butter mixture, mixing until just combined. Fold in the white sesame seeds.
6. **Shape the Cookies**: Drop rounded tablespoons of dough onto the prepared baking sheet. Flatten each ball slightly with the back of a spoon or your fingers.
7. **Garnish (Optional)**: If desired, sprinkle additional white sesame seeds on top of each cookie before baking.
8. **Bake**: Bake in the preheated oven for 10-12 minutes, or until the edges are golden brown and the centers are set.
9. **Cool**: Allow the cookies to cool on the baking sheet for a few minutes before transferring them to a wire rack to cool completely.
10. **Enjoy**: Store in an airtight container for up to a week.

Notes:

- **Matcha Powder**: Use high-quality matcha powder for the best flavor and color. If you don't have matcha, you can use green tea powder as a substitute, but the flavor may be less intense.
- **Sesame Seeds**: Toasting the sesame seeds enhances their flavor. To toast, heat them in a dry skillet over medium heat until they become fragrant, about 3-5 minutes.

These Matcha and White Sesame Cookies are a delightful fusion of flavors and textures, perfect for a unique and elegant treat. Enjoy them with tea or as a special dessert!

Shiso and Almond Cookies

Ingredients:

For the Cookies:

- 1 cup (2 sticks) unsalted butter, softened
- 1 cup granulated sugar
- 1/2 cup packed brown sugar
- 1 large egg
- 1 teaspoon vanilla extract
- 1/4 cup finely chopped fresh shiso leaves (or 2 tablespoons dried shiso powder, see notes)
- 1 3/4 cups all-purpose flour
- 1/2 teaspoon baking powder
- 1/4 teaspoon baking soda
- 1/4 teaspoon salt
- 1/2 cup finely chopped almonds (toasted if preferred)

For the Garnish (Optional):

- Extra chopped almonds for sprinkling

Instructions:

1. **Preheat Oven**: Preheat your oven to 350°F (175°C). Line a baking sheet with parchment paper or a silicone baking mat.
2. **Cream Butter and Sugars**: In a large bowl, beat the softened butter, granulated sugar, and brown sugar together until light and fluffy, about 2-3 minutes.
3. **Add Egg, Vanilla, and Shiso**: Mix in the egg, vanilla extract, and finely chopped shiso leaves (or dried shiso powder) until well combined.
4. **Mix Dry Ingredients**: In a separate bowl, whisk together the flour, baking powder, baking soda, and salt.
5. **Combine Ingredients**: Gradually add the dry ingredients to the butter mixture, mixing until just combined. Fold in the finely chopped almonds.
6. **Shape the Cookies**: Drop rounded tablespoons of dough onto the prepared baking sheet. Flatten each ball slightly with the back of a spoon or your fingers.
7. **Garnish (Optional)**: If desired, sprinkle extra chopped almonds on top of each cookie before baking.
8. **Bake**: Bake in the preheated oven for 10-12 minutes, or until the edges are golden brown and the centers are set.
9. **Cool**: Allow the cookies to cool on the baking sheet for a few minutes before transferring them to a wire rack to cool completely.
10. **Enjoy**: Store in an airtight container for up to a week.

Notes:

- **Shiso Leaves**: Fresh shiso leaves can be found at Asian markets or specialty grocery stores. Finely chop the leaves to integrate their flavor into the dough. If using dried shiso powder, adjust the quantity to taste.
- **Toasting Almonds**: Toasting the almonds enhances their flavor. To toast, heat them in a dry skillet over medium heat until they become fragrant and golden brown, about 3-5 minutes.
- **Texture**: These cookies will have a slightly crisp exterior with a tender interior, and the shiso adds a refreshing, herbal note that complements the nutty almonds.

These Shiso and Almond Cookies offer a unique blend of flavors, making them a perfect treat for those who enjoy experimenting with new and distinctive tastes. Enjoy them as a special treat or to impress guests with a unique flavor combination!

Sweet Potato and Black Sesame Cookies

Ingredients:

For the Cookies:

- 1 cup (2 sticks) unsalted butter, softened
- 1 cup granulated sugar
- 1/2 cup packed brown sugar
- 1 large egg
- 1 cup sweet potato puree (see notes for preparation)
- 1 teaspoon vanilla extract
- 2 1/4 cups all-purpose flour
- 1/2 teaspoon baking powder
- 1/4 teaspoon baking soda
- 1/4 teaspoon salt
- 1/4 cup black sesame seeds (toasted if preferred)
- 1/2 teaspoon ground cinnamon (optional, for added warmth)

For the Garnish (Optional):

- Extra black sesame seeds for sprinkling

Instructions:

1. **Preheat Oven**: Preheat your oven to 350°F (175°C). Line a baking sheet with parchment paper or a silicone baking mat.
2. **Prepare Sweet Potato Puree**: If using fresh sweet potatoes, peel and cut them into chunks. Boil or steam until tender, then mash or blend until smooth. Let it cool before using. You can also use canned sweet potato puree.
3. **Cream Butter and Sugars**: In a large bowl, beat the softened butter, granulated sugar, and brown sugar together until light and fluffy, about 2-3 minutes.
4. **Add Egg, Sweet Potato Puree, and Vanilla**: Mix in the egg, sweet potato puree, and vanilla extract until well combined.
5. **Mix Dry Ingredients**: In a separate bowl, whisk together the flour, baking powder, baking soda, salt, and ground cinnamon (if using).
6. **Combine Ingredients**: Gradually add the dry ingredients to the butter mixture, mixing until just combined. Fold in the black sesame seeds.
7. **Shape the Cookies**: Drop rounded tablespoons of dough onto the prepared baking sheet. Flatten each ball slightly with the back of a spoon or your fingers.
8. **Garnish (Optional)**: If desired, sprinkle additional black sesame seeds on top of each cookie before baking.
9. **Bake**: Bake in the preheated oven for 12-15 minutes, or until the edges are golden brown and the centers are set.

10. **Cool**: Allow the cookies to cool on the baking sheet for a few minutes before transferring them to a wire rack to cool completely.
11. **Enjoy**: Store in an airtight container for up to a week.

Notes:

- **Sweet Potato Puree**: If using canned sweet potato puree, make sure it's plain and not sweetened or spiced. Fresh sweet potatoes can be boiled or steamed until tender, then mashed or blended.
- **Toasting Sesame Seeds**: Toasting the black sesame seeds enhances their flavor. To toast, heat them in a dry skillet over medium heat until they become fragrant, about 3-5 minutes.
- **Texture**: These cookies will have a soft and slightly chewy texture with a unique flavor combination. The sweet potato adds moisture and natural sweetness, while the black sesame seeds provide a nutty crunch.

These Sweet Potato and Black Sesame Cookies are a delightful fusion of flavors and textures, perfect for those who enjoy unique and comforting treats. Enjoy them as a snack or a special dessert!

Uji Matcha and White Chocolate Chip Cookies

Ingredients:

For the Cookies:

- 1 cup (2 sticks) unsalted butter, softened
- 1 cup granulated sugar
- 1/2 cup packed brown sugar
- 1 large egg
- 1 teaspoon vanilla extract
- 2 tablespoons Uji matcha powder (high-quality preferred)
- 2 cups all-purpose flour
- 1/2 teaspoon baking powder
- 1/4 teaspoon baking soda
- 1/4 teaspoon salt
- 1 cup white chocolate chips

For the Garnish (Optional):

- Extra Uji matcha powder for dusting

Instructions:

1. **Preheat Oven**: Preheat your oven to 350°F (175°C). Line a baking sheet with parchment paper or a silicone baking mat.
2. **Cream Butter and Sugars**: In a large bowl, beat the softened butter, granulated sugar, and brown sugar together until light and fluffy, about 2-3 minutes.
3. **Add Egg, Vanilla, and Matcha**: Mix in the egg, vanilla extract, and Uji matcha powder until well combined.
4. **Mix Dry Ingredients**: In a separate bowl, whisk together the flour, baking powder, baking soda, and salt.
5. **Combine Ingredients**: Gradually add the dry ingredients to the butter mixture, mixing until just combined. Fold in the white chocolate chips.
6. **Shape the Cookies**: Drop rounded tablespoons of dough onto the prepared baking sheet. Flatten each ball slightly with the back of a spoon or your fingers.
7. **Garnish (Optional)**: If desired, lightly dust the top of each cookie with extra Uji matcha powder before baking.
8. **Bake**: Bake in the preheated oven for 10-12 minutes, or until the edges are golden brown and the centers are set. The matcha should have a vibrant green color, and the white chocolate chips will be melted and slightly golden.
9. **Cool**: Allow the cookies to cool on the baking sheet for a few minutes before transferring them to a wire rack to cool completely.
10. **Enjoy**: Store in an airtight container for up to a week.

Notes:

- **Uji Matcha**: Uji matcha is a high-quality Japanese green tea powder known for its rich flavor and vibrant color. If you can't find Uji matcha, use high-quality matcha powder as a substitute.
- **Texture**: These cookies will have a soft and chewy texture with a delightful combination of matcha's earthy flavor and the sweetness of white chocolate chips.
- **Dusting with Matcha**: Dusting with extra matcha powder before baking adds a touch of color and an additional hint of matcha flavor.

These Uji Matcha and White Chocolate Chip Cookies are a sophisticated treat with a perfect blend of flavors. They make a great addition to any cookie platter or as a special treat to enjoy with tea.

Katsuobushi (Dried Bonito Flakes) Cookies

Ingredients:

For the Cookies:

- 1 cup (2 sticks) unsalted butter, softened
- 1 cup granulated sugar
- 1/2 cup packed brown sugar
- 1 large egg
- 1 teaspoon vanilla extract
- 1 3/4 cups all-purpose flour
- 1/2 teaspoon baking powder
- 1/4 teaspoon baking soda
- 1/4 teaspoon salt
- 1/4 cup katsuobushi (dried bonito flakes), finely chopped or crushed

For the Garnish (Optional):

- Extra katsuobushi flakes for sprinkling

Instructions:

1. **Preheat Oven**: Preheat your oven to 350°F (175°C). Line a baking sheet with parchment paper or a silicone baking mat.
2. **Cream Butter and Sugars**: In a large bowl, beat the softened butter, granulated sugar, and brown sugar together until light and fluffy, about 2-3 minutes.
3. **Add Egg and Vanilla**: Mix in the egg and vanilla extract until well combined.
4. **Mix Dry Ingredients**: In a separate bowl, whisk together the flour, baking powder, baking soda, and salt.
5. **Combine Ingredients**: Gradually add the dry ingredients to the butter mixture, mixing until just combined. Fold in the katsuobushi flakes.
6. **Shape the Cookies**: Drop rounded tablespoons of dough onto the prepared baking sheet. Flatten each ball slightly with the back of a spoon or your fingers.
7. **Garnish (Optional)**: If desired, sprinkle a few extra katsuobushi flakes on top of each cookie before baking.
8. **Bake**: Bake in the preheated oven for 12-15 minutes, or until the edges are golden brown and the centers are set.
9. **Cool**: Allow the cookies to cool on the baking sheet for a few minutes before transferring them to a wire rack to cool completely.
10. **Enjoy**: Store in an airtight container for up to a week.

Notes:

- **Katsuobushi**: Katsuobushi is dried bonito flakes commonly used in Japanese cooking for adding umami flavor. You can find it in Asian grocery stores or online. Finely chop or crush the flakes to incorporate them evenly into the dough.
- **Texture and Flavor**: The addition of katsuobushi will give the cookies a savory depth that contrasts with the sweetness. The cookies will have a unique flavor profile, with the katsuobushi adding an umami kick.
- **Experiment**: If you're adventurous, you can experiment with additional savory ingredients like a touch of soy sauce or miso to enhance the umami flavor further.

These Katsuobushi Cookies offer a unique twist on traditional cookies, providing a savory-sweet experience that's sure to surprise and delight. Enjoy them as an unusual treat or a conversation starter at gatherings!

Cherry and Matcha Cookies

Ingredients:

For the Cookies:

- 1 cup (2 sticks) unsalted butter, softened
- 1 cup granulated sugar
- 1/2 cup packed brown sugar
- 1 large egg
- 1 teaspoon vanilla extract
- 2 tablespoons matcha powder (high-quality preferred)
- 2 cups all-purpose flour
- 1/2 teaspoon baking powder
- 1/4 teaspoon baking soda
- 1/4 teaspoon salt
- 1 cup dried cherries, chopped (or fresh cherries, pitted and chopped, if in season)

For the Garnish (Optional):

- Extra matcha powder for dusting

Instructions:

1. **Preheat Oven**: Preheat your oven to 350°F (175°C). Line a baking sheet with parchment paper or a silicone baking mat.
2. **Cream Butter and Sugars**: In a large bowl, beat the softened butter, granulated sugar, and brown sugar together until light and fluffy, about 2-3 minutes.
3. **Add Egg, Vanilla, and Matcha**: Mix in the egg, vanilla extract, and matcha powder until well combined.
4. **Mix Dry Ingredients**: In a separate bowl, whisk together the flour, baking powder, baking soda, and salt.
5. **Combine Ingredients**: Gradually add the dry ingredients to the butter mixture, mixing until just combined. Fold in the chopped cherries.
6. **Shape the Cookies**: Drop rounded tablespoons of dough onto the prepared baking sheet. Flatten each ball slightly with the back of a spoon or your fingers.
7. **Garnish (Optional)**: If desired, lightly dust the tops of the cookies with extra matcha powder before baking.
8. **Bake**: Bake in the preheated oven for 10-12 minutes, or until the edges are golden brown and the centers are set. The cookies will have a vibrant green color with specks of red from the cherries.
9. **Cool**: Allow the cookies to cool on the baking sheet for a few minutes before transferring them to a wire rack to cool completely.
10. **Enjoy**: Store in an airtight container for up to a week.

Notes:

- **Matcha Powder**: Use high-quality matcha powder for the best flavor and color. If you can't find high-quality matcha, opt for a good-grade matcha powder to ensure the best taste.
- **Cherries**: Dried cherries work well and provide a concentrated sweetness and chewiness. If using fresh cherries, make sure they are well-drained and chopped to prevent excess moisture in the dough.
- **Texture**: These cookies will have a slightly soft and chewy texture with a beautiful contrast between the sweet cherries and the earthy matcha flavor.

These Cherry and Matcha Cookies are a visually stunning and delicious treat that perfectly balances sweet and savory flavors. Enjoy them with tea or as a unique addition to any cookie platter!

Miso and Chocolate Cookies

Ingredients:

For the Cookies:

- 1 cup (2 sticks) unsalted butter, softened
- 1 cup granulated sugar
- 1/2 cup packed brown sugar
- 1 large egg
- 1 teaspoon vanilla extract
- 1/4 cup white miso paste (mild or sweet miso is preferred)
- 2 cups all-purpose flour
- 1/2 teaspoon baking powder
- 1/4 teaspoon baking soda
- 1/4 teaspoon salt
- 1 cup semi-sweet chocolate chips or chopped chocolate

For the Garnish (Optional):

- Flaky sea salt for sprinkling

Instructions:

1. **Preheat Oven**: Preheat your oven to 350°F (175°C). Line a baking sheet with parchment paper or a silicone baking mat.
2. **Cream Butter and Sugars**: In a large bowl, beat the softened butter, granulated sugar, and brown sugar together until light and fluffy, about 2-3 minutes.
3. **Add Egg, Vanilla, and Miso**: Mix in the egg, vanilla extract, and white miso paste until well combined. The miso will add a subtle savory depth to the dough.
4. **Mix Dry Ingredients**: In a separate bowl, whisk together the flour, baking powder, baking soda, and salt.
5. **Combine Ingredients**: Gradually add the dry ingredients to the butter mixture, mixing until just combined. Fold in the chocolate chips or chopped chocolate.
6. **Shape the Cookies**: Drop rounded tablespoons of dough onto the prepared baking sheet. Flatten each ball slightly with the back of a spoon or your fingers.
7. **Garnish (Optional)**: If desired, sprinkle a small pinch of flaky sea salt on top of each cookie before baking. This will enhance the flavors and add a touch of sophistication.
8. **Bake**: Bake in the preheated oven for 10-12 minutes, or until the edges are golden brown and the centers are set. The cookies will have a slightly crisp edge with a soft center.
9. **Cool**: Allow the cookies to cool on the baking sheet for a few minutes before transferring them to a wire rack to cool completely.
10. **Enjoy**: Store in an airtight container for up to a week.

Notes:

- **Miso Paste**: Use white miso (also called sweet miso) for a milder flavor. If using a stronger miso, start with a smaller amount and adjust to taste.
- **Texture and Flavor**: The miso adds a subtle umami flavor that complements the sweetness of the chocolate. The result is a cookie with a complex and intriguing taste.
- **Sea Salt**: Adding flaky sea salt on top before baking enhances the cookies' flavor by balancing the sweetness with a touch of saltiness.

These Miso and Chocolate Cookies are a delightful twist on classic chocolate cookies, offering a unique flavor experience that combines sweet, savory, and umami notes. Enjoy them with a cup of tea or as a special treat!

Wasabi and Cashew Cookies

Ingredients:

For the Cookies:

- 1 cup (2 sticks) unsalted butter, softened
- 1 cup granulated sugar
- 1/2 cup packed brown sugar
- 1 large egg
- 1 teaspoon vanilla extract
- 1 tablespoon wasabi paste (adjust to taste)
- 2 cups all-purpose flour
- 1/2 teaspoon baking powder
- 1/4 teaspoon baking soda
- 1/4 teaspoon salt
- 1/2 cup chopped cashews (toasted if preferred)

For the Garnish (Optional):

- Extra chopped cashews for sprinkling

Instructions:

1. **Preheat Oven**: Preheat your oven to 350°F (175°C). Line a baking sheet with parchment paper or a silicone baking mat.
2. **Cream Butter and Sugars**: In a large bowl, beat the softened butter, granulated sugar, and brown sugar together until light and fluffy, about 2-3 minutes.
3. **Add Egg, Vanilla, and Wasabi**: Mix in the egg, vanilla extract, and wasabi paste until well combined. Start with 1 tablespoon of wasabi paste and adjust according to your spice preference.
4. **Mix Dry Ingredients**: In a separate bowl, whisk together the flour, baking powder, baking soda, and salt.
5. **Combine Ingredients**: Gradually add the dry ingredients to the butter mixture, mixing until just combined. Fold in the chopped cashews.
6. **Shape the Cookies**: Drop rounded tablespoons of dough onto the prepared baking sheet. Flatten each ball slightly with the back of a spoon or your fingers.
7. **Garnish (Optional)**: If desired, sprinkle extra chopped cashews on top of each cookie before baking.
8. **Bake**: Bake in the preheated oven for 10-12 minutes, or until the edges are golden brown and the centers are set.
9. **Cool**: Allow the cookies to cool on the baking sheet for a few minutes before transferring them to a wire rack to cool completely.
10. **Enjoy**: Store in an airtight container for up to a week.

Notes:

- **Wasabi Paste**: Wasabi paste can vary in strength. Start with 1 tablespoon and taste the dough to adjust if needed. If using wasabi powder, mix it with a little water to create a paste before adding it to the dough.
- **Toasting Cashews**: Toasting the cashews enhances their flavor. To toast, heat them in a dry skillet over medium heat until they become fragrant and golden brown, about 3-5 minutes.
- **Texture and Flavor**: These cookies will have a buttery, slightly crunchy texture with a surprising wasabi kick. The cashews add a rich, nutty flavor that balances the heat of the wasabi.

These Wasabi and Cashew Cookies are a bold and unique treat that pairs sweet and savory elements with a spicy twist. They're perfect for those who enjoy adventurous flavors and want to try something out of the ordinary!

Yuzu Marmalade Cookies

Ingredients:

For the Cookies:

- 1 cup (2 sticks) unsalted butter, softened
- 1 cup granulated sugar
- 1/2 cup packed brown sugar
- 1 large egg
- 1 teaspoon vanilla extract
- 1/2 cup yuzu marmalade (store-bought or homemade)
- 2 1/4 cups all-purpose flour
- 1/2 teaspoon baking powder
- 1/4 teaspoon baking soda
- 1/4 teaspoon salt

For the Garnish (Optional):

- Extra yuzu marmalade for drizzling or spreading
- Powdered sugar for dusting

Instructions:

1. **Preheat Oven**: Preheat your oven to 350°F (175°C). Line a baking sheet with parchment paper or a silicone baking mat.
2. **Cream Butter and Sugars**: In a large bowl, beat the softened butter, granulated sugar, and brown sugar together until light and fluffy, about 2-3 minutes.
3. **Add Egg, Vanilla, and Yuzu Marmalade**: Mix in the egg, vanilla extract, and yuzu marmalade until well combined.
4. **Mix Dry Ingredients**: In a separate bowl, whisk together the flour, baking powder, baking soda, and salt.
5. **Combine Ingredients**: Gradually add the dry ingredients to the butter mixture, mixing until just combined.
6. **Shape the Cookies**: Drop rounded tablespoons of dough onto the prepared baking sheet. Flatten each ball slightly with the back of a spoon or your fingers.
7. **Garnish (Optional)**: If desired, lightly drizzle or spread a small amount of extra yuzu marmalade on top of each cookie before baking. You can also dust with powdered sugar after baking for a finishing touch.
8. **Bake**: Bake in the preheated oven for 10-12 minutes, or until the edges are golden brown and the centers are set.
9. **Cool**: Allow the cookies to cool on the baking sheet for a few minutes before transferring them to a wire rack to cool completely.
10. **Enjoy**: Store in an airtight container for up to a week.

Notes:

- **Yuzu Marmalade**: Yuzu marmalade can be found in Asian grocery stores or specialty markets. If you don't have access to yuzu marmalade, you can substitute with a lemon or orange marmalade, though the flavor will be slightly different.
- **Texture**: These cookies will have a soft and slightly chewy texture with a refreshing citrus flavor from the yuzu marmalade.
- **Extra Marmalade**: Drizzling or spreading extra yuzu marmalade on top before baking adds an extra layer of citrus sweetness and makes the cookies look more appealing.

These Yuzu Marmalade Cookies are a delightful treat that perfectly combines the unique flavor of yuzu with a classic cookie base. Enjoy them with a cup of tea or as a special dessert!

Sweet Red Bean and Chestnut Cookies

Ingredients:

For the Cookies:

- 1 cup (2 sticks) unsalted butter, softened
- 1 cup granulated sugar
- 1/2 cup packed brown sugar
- 1 large egg
- 1 teaspoon vanilla extract
- 1/2 cup sweet red bean paste (anko), smooth or chunky
- 1 cup cooked chestnuts, finely chopped (or canned chestnuts, drained and chopped)
- 2 1/4 cups all-purpose flour
- 1/2 teaspoon baking powder
- 1/4 teaspoon baking soda
- 1/4 teaspoon salt

For the Garnish (Optional):

- Extra chopped chestnuts for sprinkling
- Powdered sugar for dusting

Instructions:

1. **Preheat Oven**: Preheat your oven to 350°F (175°C). Line a baking sheet with parchment paper or a silicone baking mat.
2. **Cream Butter and Sugars**: In a large bowl, beat the softened butter, granulated sugar, and brown sugar together until light and fluffy, about 2-3 minutes.
3. **Add Egg, Vanilla, and Red Bean Paste**: Mix in the egg, vanilla extract, and sweet red bean paste until well combined. The red bean paste adds a unique flavor and moisture to the dough.
4. **Mix Dry Ingredients**: In a separate bowl, whisk together the flour, baking powder, baking soda, and salt.
5. **Combine Ingredients**: Gradually add the dry ingredients to the butter mixture, mixing until just combined. Fold in the chopped chestnuts.
6. **Shape the Cookies**: Drop rounded tablespoons of dough onto the prepared baking sheet. Flatten each ball slightly with the back of a spoon or your fingers.
7. **Garnish (Optional)**: If desired, sprinkle a few extra chopped chestnuts on top of each cookie before baking. You can also dust with powdered sugar after baking for an extra touch.
8. **Bake**: Bake in the preheated oven for 12-15 minutes, or until the edges are golden brown and the centers are set.

9. **Cool**: Allow the cookies to cool on the baking sheet for a few minutes before transferring them to a wire rack to cool completely.
10. **Enjoy**: Store in an airtight container for up to a week.

Notes:

- **Sweet Red Bean Paste**: You can use store-bought sweet red bean paste (anko) or make your own from adzuki beans. If using homemade paste, ensure it's smooth and free of large bean pieces unless you prefer a chunkier texture.
- **Chestnuts**: Use cooked chestnuts for the best flavor. If using canned chestnuts, make sure to drain and chop them finely. Roasting fresh chestnuts before using will enhance their flavor.
- **Texture and Flavor**: These cookies will have a tender and slightly chewy texture with a delightful mix of sweet red bean and nutty chestnut flavors.
- **Powdered Sugar**: Dusting with powdered sugar after baking adds a touch of sweetness and a polished look to the cookies.

These Sweet Red Bean and Chestnut Cookies are a wonderful fusion of traditional Japanese ingredients with classic cookie-making techniques. They offer a unique and tasty experience that's sure to impress!

Japanese Pear Cookies

Ingredients:

For the Cookies:

- 1 cup (2 sticks) unsalted butter, softened
- 1 cup granulated sugar
- 1/2 cup packed brown sugar
- 1 large egg
- 1 teaspoon vanilla extract
- 1 cup finely grated Japanese pear (peeled and cored; about 1 medium pear)
- 2 1/4 cups all-purpose flour
- 1/2 teaspoon baking powder
- 1/4 teaspoon baking soda
- 1/4 teaspoon salt
- 1/2 teaspoon ground cinnamon (optional, for extra warmth)

For the Garnish (Optional):

- Extra granulated sugar for sprinkling
- Pear slices for decoration (optional)

Instructions:

1. **Preheat Oven**: Preheat your oven to 350°F (175°C). Line a baking sheet with parchment paper or a silicone baking mat.
2. **Prepare Pear**: Peel and core the Japanese pear, then grate it finely. Squeeze out excess moisture using a paper towel or cheesecloth to ensure the dough doesn't become too wet.
3. **Cream Butter and Sugars**: In a large bowl, beat the softened butter, granulated sugar, and brown sugar together until light and fluffy, about 2-3 minutes.
4. **Add Egg, Vanilla, and Pear**: Mix in the egg, vanilla extract, and grated pear until well combined. The pear adds moisture and a subtle fruitiness to the dough.
5. **Mix Dry Ingredients**: In a separate bowl, whisk together the flour, baking powder, baking soda, salt, and ground cinnamon (if using).
6. **Combine Ingredients**: Gradually add the dry ingredients to the butter mixture, mixing until just combined. The dough should be soft and slightly sticky.
7. **Shape the Cookies**: Drop rounded tablespoons of dough onto the prepared baking sheet. Flatten each ball slightly with the back of a spoon or your fingers. If using pear slices for decoration, place a small slice on top of each cookie.
8. **Garnish (Optional)**: If desired, lightly sprinkle the tops of the cookies with extra granulated sugar before baking. This adds a touch of sweetness and a slight crunch.

9. **Bake**: Bake in the preheated oven for 12-15 minutes, or until the edges are golden brown and the centers are set. The cookies will have a soft and slightly chewy texture.
10. **Cool**: Allow the cookies to cool on the baking sheet for a few minutes before transferring them to a wire rack to cool completely.
11. **Enjoy**: Store in an airtight container for up to a week.

Notes:

- **Japanese Pear**: Japanese pears (nashi) have a crisp and juicy texture. If you can't find Japanese pears, you can substitute with any firm, sweet pear, but adjust the moisture content in the dough as needed.
- **Texture**: The cookies should be soft and slightly chewy, with the pear adding a delicate sweetness and moisture.
- **Decoration**: Adding pear slices on top of the cookies before baking enhances their appearance and adds an extra burst of pear flavor.

These Japanese Pear Cookies are a wonderful way to showcase the unique flavor of Japanese pears. Enjoy them as a special treat with tea or as a delightful addition to any dessert spread!

Kinako and Matcha Shortbread Cookies

Ingredients:

For the Cookies:

- 1 cup (2 sticks) unsalted butter, softened
- 1/2 cup granulated sugar
- 1/4 cup powdered sugar
- 1 cup all-purpose flour
- 1/2 cup kinako (roasted soybean flour)
- 2 tablespoons matcha powder
- 1/4 teaspoon salt

For the Garnish (Optional):

- Extra kinako or matcha powder for dusting

Instructions:

1. **Preheat Oven**: Preheat your oven to 350°F (175°C). Line a baking sheet with parchment paper or a silicone baking mat.
2. **Cream Butter and Sugars**: In a large bowl, beat the softened butter, granulated sugar, and powdered sugar together until light and fluffy, about 2-3 minutes.
3. **Mix Dry Ingredients**: In a separate bowl, whisk together the flour, kinako, matcha powder, and salt.
4. **Combine Ingredients**: Gradually add the dry ingredients to the butter mixture, mixing until just combined. The dough will be somewhat crumbly but should come together when pressed.
5. **Shape the Cookies**: Turn the dough out onto a lightly floured surface. Roll it out to about 1/4-inch thickness. Use cookie cutters to cut out shapes, or simply slice into squares or rectangles.
6. **Transfer and Bake**: Place the cut-out dough onto the prepared baking sheet. If desired, sprinkle a bit of extra kinako or matcha powder on top of each cookie for added flavor and decoration.
7. **Bake**: Bake in the preheated oven for 12-15 minutes, or until the edges are lightly golden. The centers should be firm but not overly brown.
8. **Cool**: Allow the cookies to cool on the baking sheet for a few minutes before transferring them to a wire rack to cool completely.
9. **Enjoy**: Store in an airtight container for up to a week.

Notes:

- **Kinako**: Kinako adds a nutty, slightly sweet flavor that complements the rich, earthy matcha. It can be found in Asian grocery stores or online.
- **Matcha Powder**: Use high-quality matcha powder for the best flavor and color. If the matcha is too strong, you can adjust the amount to suit your taste.
- **Texture**: Shortbread cookies should be crisp and crumbly. If the dough is too dry, you can add a small amount of milk or water to help it come together.
- **Decoration**: The optional kinako or matcha powder dusting on top adds visual appeal and extra flavor. You can also dip half of each cookie in melted chocolate for an additional touch.

These Kinako and Matcha Shortbread Cookies offer a unique and flavorful twist on classic shortbread, combining traditional Japanese ingredients for a deliciously different treat. Enjoy them with tea or as a special dessert!

Japanese Chestnut and Ginger Cookies

Ingredients:

For the Cookies:

1 cup (2 sticks) unsalted butter, softened

1 cup granulated sugar

1/2 cup packed brown sugar

1 large egg

1 teaspoon vanilla extract

1 cup cooked chestnuts, finely chopped (or canned chestnuts, drained and chopped)

2 tablespoons ground ginger

2 1/4 cups all-purpose flour

1/2 teaspoon baking powder

1/4 teaspoon baking soda

1/4 teaspoon salt

For the Garnish (Optional):

Extra granulated sugar for sprinkling

Crystallized ginger pieces, finely chopped

Instructions:

Preheat Oven: Preheat your oven to 350°F (175°C). Line a baking sheet with parchment paper or a silicone baking mat.

Cream Butter and Sugars: In a large bowl, beat the softened butter, granulated sugar, and brown sugar together until light and fluffy, about 2-3 minutes.

Add Egg and Vanilla: Mix in the egg and vanilla extract until well combined.

Add Chestnuts and Ginger: Stir in the finely chopped chestnuts and ground ginger until evenly distributed.

Mix Dry Ingredients: In a separate bowl, whisk together the flour, baking powder, baking soda, and salt.

Combine Ingredients: Gradually add the dry ingredients to the butter mixture, mixing until just combined.

Shape the Cookies: Drop rounded tablespoons of dough onto the prepared baking sheet. Flatten each ball slightly with the back of a spoon or your fingers.

Garnish (Optional): If desired, sprinkle a little granulated sugar on top of each cookie and add finely chopped crystallized ginger for extra flavor and decoration.

Bake: Bake in the preheated oven for 12-15 minutes, or until the edges are golden brown and the centers are set. The cookies should be soft in the middle with a crisp edge.

Cool: Allow the cookies to cool on the baking sheet for a few minutes before transferring them to a wire rack to cool completely.

Enjoy: Store in an airtight container for up to a week.

Notes:

Chestnuts: Use cooked chestnuts for the best flavor. Canned chestnuts are a convenient option, but make sure to chop them finely so they mix well into the dough. Roasting fresh chestnuts beforehand will enhance their flavor.

Ground Ginger: Adjust the amount of ground ginger according to your taste. If you prefer a milder flavor, you can start with 1 tablespoon and add more if desired.

Crystallized Ginger: Adding finely chopped crystallized ginger on top before baking enhances the cookie's flavor and adds a nice texture contrast.

Texture: These cookies will be slightly chewy with a nice crunch around the edges, and the chestnuts will add a delightful nutty flavor.

These Japanese Chestnut and Ginger Cookies are a delightful fusion of sweet and spicy flavors, making them a unique and enjoyable treat. They're perfect for special occasions or as a sophisticated addition to your cookie collection.